Under the Blue Roof

UNDER
THE
BLUE
ROOF

Edited by
Quazi J. Islam

Under the Blue Roof

Poetry Anthology

Edited by **Quazi J. Islam**

Copyright © 2018 Author(s)

Translation Copyright © 2018 Translator(s)

A painting of artist Raghib Ahsan is used for cover design

Layout and cover design by Quazi J. Islam

Price US$30.00 [or equivalent other currency]

ISBN 9781719828581

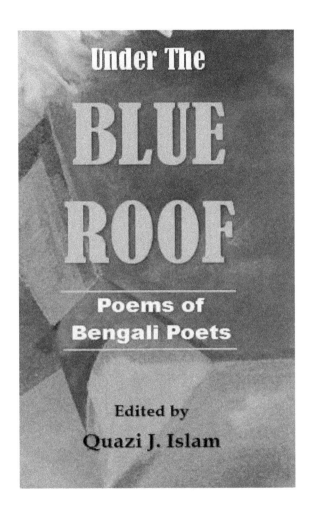

Under The

BLUE

ROOF

Poems of
Bengali Poets

Edited by

Quazi J. Islam

Editor's Note

Poets of this anthology are originally from Bangladesh; their first language is Bangla and all of them write in Bangla. Every language has its own expression that comes from the culture of soil, which is unique and can't be translated. Most of poems of this anthology are translated from Bangla, so, the original expression, in most cases, are lost; we must admit it. My humble request to readers, please read this anthology keeping that in mind. In this anthology there are very powerful Bengali poets, who are already established and famous, at the same time there are young and promising poets too.

Modern Bengali poets love to hide the message of poems folded in hard shell. They believe the message they want to convey is not the message said in the poem, but there are very strong hints, so, readers may find a door to go deep inside it and find the folded message, that is the beauty of modern Bangla poems. The anthology, 'Under the Blue Roof', is a good blend of prominent and promising poets. The common ground for everyone is they all live abroad and they all miss their motherland, so we hear the music of pain in their words for beloved motherland, Bangladesh that comes from the bottom of their hearts.

Does a poet should follow any rules? The answer is a big 'No'. But a true poet knows all the rules. Rules are for poems not at all the other way around. A poet must be free and brave to break rules and tell the truth.

In this anthology we didn't follow any usual order, such as seniority or alphabetic order, poems are placed randomly, but at some point, as an editor I was trying to find a rational and I got it, yes, there is an order... the first come first serve order. Should we not respect the person who took it seriously and put maximum efforts to submit stuff on time? I think we should and that is the order has been maintained in this book.

As far as I know this is the first time such an anthology of Bangladeshi diaspora poets is being published. I have tried to accommodate as much as possible, without being selective. So, this book is not a true representation of the quality of Bangla poems but I feel proud that we have started our journey and from now on we would be able to publish often and be more selective on quality.

Quazi J. Islam
New York, USA

INDEX

U

V

Z

Dedicated to

Rafiq, Salam, Barkat,

Jabbar, Safiur, Ohiullah,

Awal and all other

unknown language martyrs

who sacrificed their

lives in Bangla Language

movement of 1952.

MAHBOOB HASAN

Date of Birth: 28 April 1954

Place of Birth: Tangail, Bangladesh

Education: PhD in Bangla Literature [Poetry]

Publication: 55

Lives in: New York, USA.

Email: poetmahbub03@yahoo.com

TO EAT OR NOT TO EAT

As human beings devour nature
And thus, go on living;
As a calf sucks milk from nip of the cow
I shall relish sun.

Like an aero plane
Sun is swirling on my head,
I shall eat that sun, with all its flesh and bone.
As the air hostesses wear Hawaiian
Slippers from the grill of the sky,
ascend on the thirsty aerodrome's
Dark runway through the wet thigh of clouds
I will come out on the lamenting foot path
Like a whistling mourning dove
I sun drenched April.
Like the pieces of a water melon
Pierced by the knife of disheveled wind
In my windy heart fresh and red
Will return, will return
With the neck of a beautiful lady.

Will eat,

The lightning fast hood of a cobra,

The tasteful heart of a bird.

Like the cold drink in the dark

and cloudy chamber of a freeze

Shall keep my mouth in a sunny sleep

Will eat all beauty like a lecher,

Will eat the snowy tip of woman's breast;

No, no, I will not take, this cliché age old white rice,

This is now fodder of ordinary people

Salt of idle noon is stored in it,

Wreckage of life;

I want,

In the menu of lunch let there by

words from the eyes of a Dow,

Like the withering yellow foliage's

Let my plate be full of vegetables

In the moaning of the golden morning.

Still all on a sudden like the pinch of fork

People will be shred in pieces

Like a shining Hilsa[1] the teeth of a tractor.

Instead of sparrow in a water-logged water

Shrill whistle of speed boat is heard.

I know in grass and hyacinth

a power pump is submerged

Its big black mouth is lurking like an instinct killer

As if it will jump right at this hour;

And it looks like a blood spilled, mute silence.

No, I will never eat

this white rice food of the commoner

Nor I want to see

The darkness of crippled hands.

Let the mouth of people

Survive the push of bending horns of rice,

Let it be drenched by the gravy of curry;

I want

Lamentation of teenager's curving eye-brows

Only thus can be eaten this

monkey faced sun of the noon.

---

[1] Bangladeshi national fish

NAY

By this negative word 'nay'
I can stir your heart, but I will not.
I am spoiled by the red glow
of Krishnachura[2] of your eyes
And the smiles of day break,
I long to see the eyes of a cute
smiling teenager in your eyes,
Radiant rays like slumber of a baby, and
And want to see hide and
seek game in our yard of tiny tots
In a moonlit night.

'Nay' is an ugly word and I want to sweep from it
My love like a small but dear dream.

I want to extract little essence of love
From your unwillingness,
Like the strong and artistic beak of a sparrow
I want to take love as from the

---

[2] Bangladeshi flower, red in colour.

venom of snake

I want lethal love

Like the lanky body of a village teen ager

I want undaunted love.

From your negative frame of mind

Like a kingfisher I want to snatch

your heart in a sudden swoop.

And I want

This urge of mine is without any blemish.

FOR YOU

Today a beautiful Sunday
of the last part of twentieth century
Is spilling out through the five fingers of mine
As the moments of agony of Afghan guerrillas pass
With psalm of death in the smell of gunfire,
And thus, lays prostate loving man.
In this time of unconquered sun dial
I am spending moments of my golden days;
But you know though
Entire water body of West Asia and the world
Is now dancing to the tune of armaments, and
Are spreading wings like bomber from Kitty Hawk
On the native shore
In adverse wind.

FOR SHAHEED QUADRI

I have you in my mind;
That year you left the
rugged city before the winter was out
And went to village;
You went out hunting bird
But was caught in the mystery web of nature;
Keeping the eerie silent window of nature open
Barren rice field spread it towards the horizon,
Winter seated tight like white flakes of cold
On the bunch of withered hay across the field,
And you at night standing
on near the house of the village chief
was watching all these, and
Heard on the roof of the
house wailing of birds hit by bullet;
That night you could not sleep.
You are in my mind;
That time while returning from the village
Keeping your cheek on the window of the train
You were engrossed in the eyes of Shaswati,
You had no bullet ridden bird in your hands,

In the corner of your glasses with drop of tear
Grey feather of a wild duck mingled together.

You are in my mind;
Your used to urbane eyes in a windy night
Like a hanging verandah engulfed in darkness
Was shedding tears,
In grief and agony,
That night you tried to spread your wings like flies
In sheer disgust with life,
Wanted to jump from the balcony of second floor
Like gusty wind of summer days,
You called 'Moyeen'
Like the trembling sound of
Azan chanted by a man frightened by storm,
You devoured moonlight like a possessed one.

One day hearing me say,
I love a girl thin and lanky with glasses on
You protested the word 'lanky',
And said, women are eloquent
And are as simple as nature is'.
I did not agree but remembered what you said.

I kept you in mind;

After the deluge, folding the trousers

With shoes in my hand on the foot path

I remembered you who was grafted in my mind.

I have remembered you

Like the memory of the fool

whose trouser is entangled in a knot

I have remembered you who is embedded in my mind.

But with a long coat on in that country of cold

Where are you now going Quadri?

WELCOME, TWO SUPERPOWERS

Like two superpowers

I also like to strike a secret dear with you,

Neither in a mega city,

Nor in a sound proof beautiful house

On the floor of an ordinary house

Sitting on a mat face to face

Without stamp with security thread

In the pattern of nuclear nonproliferation deal

We, meaning you and me

Two mental mighty powers

Signing a secret deal

Want to do away with our strategic warfare,

In the deep seat of heart, want to knit without a thread;

Only, this way we can put at rest

Our mental clash.

Come, let we love each other

Like two superpowers

On top of our warfare like a truce

Let us hoist the flag of truce6 of the century.

TO THE SEA

Then you keep your bag here,
Wind is blowing fast
On the red carpet is seated the crimson game
Obstacle removed by sun
You will lie prostrate in presence
Let the evening hang
In the yawning of the shark.

In the landscape two sea gulls
Or something else?
Touching the edge of water
Comes the foamy huge fish
On the shore beside the onlookers;
Cypress and shells wait for
Ripples on the shore.

You are immortal with all these
Avoiding the shore
How far of the sea have you seen?
Mighty roar of the sea keeps open the wind-mill,
Ceaseless water tap

Keep on pouring idleness.

You see only the red carpet, O charming hound,

You pull up the master in distress on your shoulder,

Feel pungent smell of sun in your nostrils,

You understand different signs of the master

But do not know yourself

Do not know why your master

is glued to the turbulent sea

And captive of a killing shark.

INJURED GOD

Breaking the window pane flies away the deity

Its celestial wings with ornamental decoration adorned

May be

The God of wrath

In the guise of an injured lark

Came down

Like an apostle

In us by lane

And then being

Captive

Dismantled hill

Old house

Touched heavenly leaves

Thus

The injured God

Collected

News on us.

TO A NIGHT

Like a Jasmine from your heart
A drop of morning will fall,
Standing underneath a young banyan tree
I will witness that great spectacle;
The first moment of your birth will be
Heralded by hand clapping
Like the first beloved of a maiden,
Then with you will go to pluck
song of leaves of autumn,
Will go to pluck watery weeds
like the smile of a village girl.
Still the light and wind of this world grow old.
When I will return, will see dew
of the road withered off
Jasmine lie on road high and dry
Will see the sun lit city rise
like an obstinate cobra's hood.
That freshly risen morning light
Why return to our spoilt soul?
In our rotten heart?
Why this coming back?

AMNESIA

My youth

I have seen through the window of my mind

Like a disheveled match of boys

Shameless like a temporary goal post,

Flag of the linesman.

My entire childhood

Are only the garden of Bakul trees, sound of Azan

Charmed look of a child.

But those captivating tunes of youth

I cannot bring back to my mind.

TROTTING

Why do I tie up trotting with meters?

In my blood is the call to wander

In the villages around me and in field of childhood

All peeping in my mind,

take me back to childhood days

I want to know who have spoiled all my days

Why did I tie up trotting in meters

Make a new trend in my blood.

[Translated by Fakhruzzaman Chowdhury]

MASUD KHAN

Date of Birth: 29 May 1959

Place of Birth: Joypurhat, Bangladesh

Education: B.SC in Engineering and MBA

Publication: 11

Lives in: Toronto, Canada.

Email: masud_khan@yahoo.com

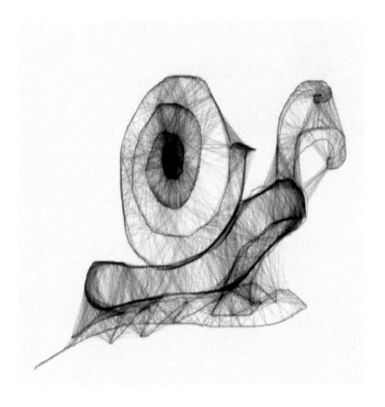

HOMA-BIRD

Once I fall, how much must I drop down before I can rise again?

As this thought crosses my mind I am reminded of the Homa bird found high in the sky. It even lays its eggs there. The eggs then fall. But because the bird lives so high in the sky its eggs take ages to fall. Its chicks hatch even as the eggs descend. And then it's time for the chicks to fall. As they begin to fall the chicks sprout eyes and feathers and wings. And one day they discover that they are falling and down. It is then that they begin to fly to their mothers' high up in the sky. They fly so high now that they emerge as specks scattered all along the spread-out body of the sky.

We are of the breed of these birds. We procreate, raise children; we drop down and rise again!

[*Homapakhi;* Translated by Fakrul Alam]

SEASON OF AFFLICTION

It was the time of seasonal change— the time to shed skins. The two of us opted to be part of some conspicuous catastrophe. But before we could do so you contracted fever. It raged so in you! Clasping the thermometer's mercury column, you ascended swiftly, climbing up, up and up, Fahrenheit degree by degree— one hundred and five, six, seven, eight... till you scaled the height of fever. You became the coefficient of the highest degree— all aflame! — till there were no more heights to climb, no more thermal coefficient, no more degrees left on the thermometer for you to conquer! And having climbed the peak of desire, the thermometer exploded, ejaculating a simmering liquid fire.

Even raging, all-consuming fevers will not destroy women. All they do is make them look somewhat more awe-inspiring— like incarnations of the goddess Kali— the more beautiful, the more awe-inspiring when raging....

And came a time when making the lidless thermometer a broomstick that you could fly on, you began to disappear into some dim disaster, my dearest witch!

For the first time in my life, I experienced such definite disaster.

The thermometer's crater was still drip-dripping steaming magma.

[*Jwarer Hritute;* Translated by Fakrul Alam]

FIRE ENGINE

Having fled the madhouse, the lunatic
darted up the tree.
Nothing would make him come down, he said,
Except for the pleas of that midget-size nurse!
The nurse came running, quick as a fire engine,
Waving wildly at him.
Her gestures were coded messages
Inducing the lunatic to climb down from the tree top
Just as a *koi* fish descends on the dining plate
Entranced by the smell of steaming curry,
He descended easily and freely
As consecutive numbers do when one counts down.
The lunatic's thoughts
flickered across the nurse's consciousness.
This day that mad man will
return once more to his asylum.
Placing his head on the confessional,
He will soundlessly suffer thirteen electric shocks
Designed to induce thirteen confessions from him
At the directive of the calm and composed health priest!

[*Damkal;* Translated by Fakrul Alam]

MOTHER

In the dust smeared evening
Far away, almost at the margins of the horizon,
The one who is resting all by herself
In a bed laid out under the open sky
Is my mother.
Her bed smells of grass and the antiseptic Dettol.
A tube in her nose supplies her with oxygen,
A saline bottle is attached to her arm,
And she is tied to a catheter too —
It is as if she is getting entangled inextricably
In a jungle of plastic and polythene reeds.
A smoky surreal unreal canopy encircles her bed.
Seemingly after ages, dusk descends on the world,
A few birds and insects form a chorus,
Wailing throatily obscure and dissonant tunes
In amateurish over-excited zeal,
Seeking refuge timorously in that plastic hedge,
At the margin of the horizon,
In the shadow of primeval motherhood.

[*Ma*; Translated by Fakrul Alam]

HISTORY

How then can an authentic history of the world be written? The one who writes— who is he and where is he writing from? When is he writing? From which vantage point is he writing and for what reason? All these factors will decide the truth of the history. And in any case the subject itself is bound by its own conventions and is inevitably subjective.

Is it then impossible to write an authentic history of the world?

No! In the light already reflected from the surface of the world till now is impressed the history of the world— chronologically! Which is to say, the history of the world is in the light dispersed from the world. And that must be authentic version of the history of the world since it's being written naturally. Perhaps in kingdom after kingdom of the cosmos someone or the other is sighting that history through telescopes, unknown to us all.

But will such a history be absolutely authentic? What about the chapters of history that are dark and depressing? Of episodes that have been denuded of light and have become shrouded in darkness and decadence? Of episodes that have never exuded light and will never reflect any radiance anywhere? What about them?

And what about the history of people who are dark or tan brown?

Perhaps their evolution has become blurred in the lenses of telescopes; perhaps their histories have become obscure in the telling— since they are dark and tan brown; perhaps because they are able to transmit only a feeble light they are deemed to be totally incapable of reflecting any light at all!

Does this mean that the history of dark and tan brown people will remain obscure forever in the history of mankind? And in nature? Bereft of light and therefore of history too?

[*Itihas;* Translated by Fakrul Alam]

FORLORN

Millions of miles up above in space
In an unmanned floating space station
A station master reported for duty.

One fine morning, a rocket dropped him off there
Along with lots and lots of his bags and baggage.
After refueling it took off again
for who knows which sky...
All of this happened such a long time ago!

Consigned to a fate colder and quieter than death
The station master now sups, sleeps, lives alone—
weightless, in a stupor from time to time
he put on his space suit and swims in space
Though tied to the station's mast all the while
With a long metal-tinsel tail.

At times, frustrated and piqued, he has a shit in space
His feces coalesce, becoming translucent and aromatic,
While his piss ends up glittering in that vast expanse.

Nobody anywhere— far or near

No ghosts or witches or genies or fairies
No angels or devils let alone gods or goddesses,
With whom could he chat or have a cup of coffee,
Not even the slightest chance
of him fearing someone!
All he can do is
commune with himself and masturbate,
Or pick a fight with himself
or have fun at his own expense
Or keep entertaining himself
playing snakes and ladders, or other board games!

A forlorn night-caressing, multi-colored fragrant
Queen in bloom— light years away!

[*Nissango;* Translated by Fakrul Alam]

DESIGN

Where ten roads cross one another before dissolving into ten different horizons, there my mother sits. From the roadside she watches the multitude, their coming and going. Some roads bring in missing men; some exhibit the forlorn, decayed, extinguishing faces of the children of Adam; some, on the other hand, show the very vibrant men and women under the shadows of the nimbus and the Twins.

One day on the bustling roadside my mother found my brother (I had yet to come to this mother then). But after a while, that brother of mine got lost. Since then, sitting at the junction of the roads, my mother shed secret tears for her lost son.

Then one day an elderly pedestrian with long dusk-coloured hair and beard stopped by her for a while. Having learned my mother's story he said, "My daughter, nothing gets lost forever in this universe. Look hard and you'll find it." And from then on, my mother had been on flight across the world, scrutinizing all its corners and niches for her son, before she found me beyond the seventh sky. She brought me to this dusty earth, believing I was the lost one. Ever before that, like an orphan, I'd been crying all alone lying in a golden haystack beside the infinite bushes of galaxies for my lost mother.

Days and months will pass by, years will roll away... I wonder how long it will be before I get lost again from this new mother only to be found by another that would have lost her son...

This eternal blunder and
bondage,

This cosmic comedy of
errors,

The secret lamentations, the lost-and-
found games,

The endless illusions and magic...

Keeping all this unresolved,

With a dirty, tattered, duplicate blueprint of the world spread out in front

Sits an ever-perplexed and indifferent Surveyor.

On one side of the blueprint is written:
Signature...(illegible),

Below it an even more indistinct seal...

[*Chhak;* Translated by Subrata Augustine Gomes]

DREAMLAND

O the home-bound sailor,
O the shaven-headed foreign captain,
tell us about the island
where leaves of money plants and solar plants
reciprocate "cheers!" and engage in competition
on drinking sunlight champagne.
Which generation do they toast to?

Tell us about the island
where womenfolk make their
ordinary wooden house blossom
with at least sixty-two kinds of love and affection.

O captain, tell us the story
of the land of love and affection,
where, at late night, girls of Radhikapur
walk on their way home whistling and filliping
and leaves and twigs of a smart,
young Ulatkamal in the bush nearby
harmoniously respond to them with counter fillips.

And the youngest daughter of a young wildcat,
instead of blabbering,
suddenly starts speaking articulately,
taking the island's forest chapter aback.

O captain, tell us about the land
where soil is warm and affectionate,
where people lie down on the ground
letting their whole body absorb vital geothermal energy.
Human body communicates directly with the ground
in an easy, spontaneous way.
O the home-bound captain,
O the shaven-headed senior sailor,
We, too, are sailing upstream endlessly.
Passing north, we're heading to further north.
By the caress of inclement briny air,
our sextant already went out of order.
Our compass got rusty,
telescope too. Still we're on voyage.

Is our long-cherished, adorable dreamland so far-off,
unreachable, incommunicable!?

PRANK

God has playfully thrown a stone to the Goddess.

From one end of the universe God has pitched the planet
toward the Goddess at the other end.

Through an extremely cold,
ever-expanding vacuum space
with million-degree silence,
the planet, the earthen projectile, is flying
like a tiny mass of greenish noise.

Not an ordinary projectile, it's a hyper missile indeed!
Zooming past the firefly-lit bushes
of the sky, galaxy after galaxy,
inducing wavering waves in the false ethereal expanse,
the projectile is racing with causeless joy
rotating like a stubborn missile inclined on one side,
spinning like an obsessed Beyblade
in its diurnal and annual motion,
with a smoky-complex connotation of speed —
a speed that's concurrently

curvilinear, circular, rotational,
dramatic, irascible, turbulent, chaotic and topsy-turvy.

The projectile's got tired.
Meanwhile, the Goddess, the obscure empress
surrounded by profound mystery
sitting at some unknown space-time coordinates
incessantly shows her flirty
gestures and relocates herself.

The Space is expanding continually.
The projectile's flight through
the ever-bending space and time
is scary and violent indeed,
and the terrified, hapless humans and creatures
scared of falling off the flying
mass are struggling to survive
sticking to it like fleas.

God and Goddess play a dangerous projectile game
and their kids shiver in panic and horripilation.

INSUBMISSIVE

As a ferocious lion ran past him,
a boy sans lion-driving training and license
narrowly managed to get on it is gripping its mane.
Now he can neither dismount nor stay mounted.
Dismounting is not as easy as mounting.

The inexperienced boy cannot recognize
the switch, brake, battery, gear selector...
Devoid of lion-driving skills, the confused boy,
based on assumption,
is operating one device for the other.

It's a wrong mantra, though, for hypnosis,
yet spelling it out reversely,
the boy is whiffing around on the lion's mane on and on.
Germinals of fire — jubilant, virgin — sprout instantly
wherever the whiffs touch on the mane.

Fuel is heavily burning
inside the lion's internal combustion engine.
Defying the imperatives of Carnot cycle,

pistons are randomly reciprocating inside the cylinders
along with ghostly skills of one-way valves.
Both the lion and the rider are freaking out
amid frequent farting of methane and monoxides,
recurrent misfire, random lubrication,
sporadic anaerobic combustion,
bizarre noise and odor pollution.

Surroundings and the locality get gravely afflicted.
Dismounting is not as easy as mounting.

PREACHING

You need light to walk on
a path. I'm blind, I need nothing.

I'll be heading to China, to a Zen monastery,
swaying a bamboo-leaf lantern in hand,
or, further to a faraway land.
There, sitting beneath a blossoming cherry tree,
during the preaching session,
I'll be devotedly listening to bees buzzing on the tree
and staying unmindful as
I left my mind in a faraway land.
Guru's cane will whip me at the back
leaving pure ornament-marks
that look like flowers of golden shower.

I'll take lessons on economy of speech
but gradually turn out as a garrulous speaker.
Instead of being letterless I'll be full of letters.
Floating my tummy stuffed with fun and laughter,
I'll be telling stories — sometimes
of love, sometimes of anger,

or meditation, or of profoundly fragrant Kamini flower

blossoming in the dead of night.

It'll be drizzling in the monastery's cloudy yard.

Meanwhile, the nearby field

reddened with chilies will start flaming.

This piece of info will rush

to strike my skin and membranes.

Now, as I'll be telling the story of burning chilies,

everybody, even an old man,

induced by the splash of chilly-heat,

will dash towards the battle field.

When the story of love— oranges

will start assuming their colour

amid mild, golden sunshine.

And again, as I'll be humming the fragrance-fiction

of a wet, insomniac Kamini flower,

nectar fruits inside the body will start melting

induced by the warmth of fragrance.

QUAZI JOHIRUL ISLAM

Date of Birth: 10 February 1968

Place of Birth: Brahmanbaria, Bangladesh

Education: Master of Management and CPA

Publication: 47

Lives in: New York, USA.

Email: unobangal@gmail.com

HEADLESS GENERALS

There are few headless Generals in the ablution unit.
An extreme noise in cantonment, who has done it?
How is it possible, who has that audacity?
It has been a grave issue, so many
committees are formed, tension torrent the roof.

Contentment among few
people, of course in a different den.

Shoot or hang to death, what
will be the sentence, 'prepare the firing squad'
A roar has been exploded in the court room.
Excited faces of uniformed attorneys in
front of a uniformed judge.
After a long hearing the judge opened his mouth
'where is the criminal?'
O yes, where is the criminal? And who is he?
'Why the criminal has not yet been
identified? Where is he?' Asked the Judge.
'got him, here he is…he is the one
committed that severe crime,

has cut off the elite heads of Generals' saying this
couple of new uniformed
entered the court room with a poor guy tied
up his hands in back.

All eyes of the court room now
focused on the poor guy,
status of whom is few levels below than
the bloody civilians.

The wise judge can't wait anymore,
he just shut the moth of attorneys
by his rank and shouted,
'why did you do that? Why did you cut off
the elite heads of Generals?'
'Huzur' poor guy started crying,
Da Da Da, gun shot in firing squad...

'if I wouldn't cut the heads off,
the bloody schedule-caste
would have peed on faces of the elite Generals.
To save the dignity of Generals
I have cut their heads off, Huzur.'

FOUR BOATS AND FOUR LAMPS
OF FOUR DISTINCT COLOURS

Someone shouts at the doorstep of sleep

at the end of night

'wake up Quazi's son, there are guests in the village'

Crossing the mud and fog of Karthik

a pair of hoary Kurta clapping to make rhythmic noise

in the light dark of Subeh Sadek[3].

'be careful brides and daughters

be careful men and women

there are guests in the village

be careful children'

Running towards the end of the

village two elderly men

in the tail of night when three scary boats have

landed pushing the mud of

Karthik[4]; the scares are being lit

inside the boats, three colours of lights.

---

[3] Early morning

[4] A month Bangla Callender, [15 October to 15 November]

The cholera jumped on the land with red lamp in hand,
blue lamp in hand the small pox
and sparkling yellow the Kamela[5] disease.
In a moment three Asmani[6] diseases
spread all over the village.

Every night reciting Quoran they keep
clapping, two elderly men
Keep the village of Khagatua awaken by raising zikr
'innocent brides and daughters careful
No one should name the diseases
Three lamps of lights have come to the
village, they are guests.'

Secular diseases have no resist choice
They don't pick fair beauty or black Aiburi[7]
All day coffins are running towards

---

[5] Yellow Disease [Jaundice]
[6] Something has come from the sky.
[7] The elderly girl not yet married [in Bangladeshi village it was a curse]

Gorostan[8] and Shamshan.[9]

Northern air getting heavier with the mourning.

Night crawls down to the village like a giant dark eerie

frightened Khagatua enters in a tree-hole.

And then another green boat lands in the village.

A bright green light is splashing lives from the boat

In a hurry, must save thousands,

jumped out from the boat a Hakim[10]

He runs towards deep inside the village,

touches leaves, plants, grown in kitchen gardens.

His magical hands turn every

Lau-Macha[11] as savior medicine.

Abandoned property, swamp

land, low-land, everywhere

he seedlings the savior medicine.

After passing the horror time the

---

[8] Muslim graveyard.
[9] Hindu's graveyard.
[10] Doctor
[11] Water guard [vegetable]

Sheuli[12] smiles in the morning of Agrahaon[13].

The days of Asmani is now the grass

of the grave of Jasimuddin.[14]

New panic is now awaiting in every turn of the city

Multi-color digital diseases are now

chasing everywhere.

He, our new Hakim, will come with

what colour of lamp in hand?

---

[12] Nocturnal flowers.

[13] A month of Bengali Callender [15 October to 15 November]

[14] He is a poet, titled rural poet.

WOMAN

I don't want you to be a scaffold and save my virginity.
Rather I want you to be a mason,
use your hammer hard on me, cut me into pieces
and put me in your mixer, roll it, roll it…

and build a new world…

I don't want barren virginity under a safe scaffold.

Let me speak free and loud.

NIGHT

It's not true,
I'm not sleeping.

The truth is
I've kept you awaken, naughty night.

I enjoy your beauty
more in noise than silence.

Speak to me
empty your dark body on me.

COFFEE MUG

Again, you bought me a new one, a beautiful one,
a very special one, with new features.
Not only hot tea or coffee remains hot,
in this special one, while drive I can hit cold
liquid in the car; I have lost all the mugs...

you presented me on my all birthdays, a
continuous endeavor to proof you love me so much,
you care me, I know you have bought again
and again, my favorite coffee mugs and every
time a newer, a better one and each time you
spent an affectionate lecture to explain me
all its newer and useful features.

But I know I'll lose it again and sip in your cup
as if merely I made a mistake while driving...

and again, I will remind you to use a better lipstick
that doesn't melt on my lips.

THIRTY APPLES

Recently I have got friendship with thirty fresh apples,
passing the debate of Oriana Falacci, they often
Reach to three million.

Leaving adorable character of childhood
They've formed hard shape
of adolescent, round and attractive.
Some are green, some red, golden beauty also falling
from some of their body.

Looking at their lively meeting
sometimes I feel like multi-ethnic
harmony of Jackson Heights;
girls of assorted colors
are roaming around so cheerfully;
on their bosoms the apples of bravery
and in their kiss-thirst leaps
the smile of an undivided world.

It is a routine that I meet them every morning
and we share some prominent issues

they let me know their secret plan
and they grow bigger everyday aiming to love.

But I know they are also prepared to burst.

THE TALE OF DAY AND NIGHT

Long ago, there was no color of the earth
No black, no white, no dark, no light.
Day and night were not divided
by the line of dawn and dusk.

Only there were two groups of people.
Envy at the heart of one group, they
possess darkness inside.
It was God's will, he made them such a way
so that they couldn't think anything positive,
darkness of their heart they used to throw to the earth
and that is how the dark side of the earth is created.

And the other group was kind to God's
creatures by the will of God.
They used to go across the drought and Tsunami
one land to another land to help people,
They lit the hoary light in the earth and created day.

That is how the day and the night were born.

Now also there are two groups of people in this world.
One group would like to cover the sun by envy;
and the other one lit the dark night
with the light of love.

ECLIPSE

Father, you said,
'we must complete our job before the dusk'
Same was echoed in
grandfather's voice that he heard
from the great grandfather,
who was the root of an old tree.
The same bell was rung in every morning of prospects.

Gradually this verse like holy-book
flowing towards newer generations
'we must complete our job before the dusk'
But as like as every past episode
nothing of us are done yet, O Father, look,
we haven't done anything yet, what a grave-dark
is crawling down to our independence;
it is quite visible that all our achievements
are being doomed in deep dark.

Father, I don't want to convey the same old message
to my son. Rather I would like to tell loudly
in his eardrum, son, you better learn

how to coop with darkness, because you
and your future generations
shall live in eclipse many more years.

WISHES

Wishes are growing
bigger and bigger
everyday...

now they are tall enough
to be broken down
to the ground.

IN BETWEEN

Why have they captured me?
I couldn't realise that clearly
My hands are tied in back
Feet are tied too
They have blindfolded me with black cloth
People are howling all around
I could feel obnoxious smell in my nose
Are vultures flying? I could hear death
My skin is burning at heat of naked fire
Will they burn me to ashes?

The thin line amid life and death is being erased
Any moment they might throw me to open fire
While I am embracing the death,
I could remember the face of my beloved wife
'Keep in mind, teach Agni guitar and Joal to sing.'
Brother and sister, my two beloved children,
They'll spread out my lyrics in the air.
And people will breathe in that lyrical air
And will become true lovers.

I hear a group of fierce black Africans
Are choiring and spitting on my body,
They have raised a slogan, 'kill the bloody white dog,
Burn him, smash that white dog
of the United Nations.'
Should I laugh, while embracing
this disgraceful death?
Just couple of years ago, a German damsel
Did not shake my hand, as I was black,
What a pity, in West Africa,
Today I am facing death as I am a white!
I could never capitalise the benefits
of being in-between.

My body is being slashed up by the myriad boots
And beaten by wooden clubs
I can't scream any more,
My throat is dry, tongue is listless
The blood is oozing out of lacerated skin of my body
And drenching African soil.

I feel very sleepy now
Am I passing out to the dank darkness of death, then?

But my brain is alert yet,
I could clearly reflect about my colleague
Yirgalem Gebreselassie, whose three brothers
Sacrificed their lives for the liberation of Eritrea
Where is that girl now?
She was with me
Outside city, other side of the
lagoon, crossing the jungle
We went to a devastated village
To distribute foods to the hunger-stricken people.

Did the Militias murder her already?
Or pouring down virus of hate
on her body with frenzy?

They loaded my body on a vehicle,
It is an open Jeep
I could feel piercing pain
As the summer wind biting my lacerated body.
In about two hours

They've stopped the car in a solitary desert
Then they threw my body on the desert sand

Assuming I'm dead.

They unfastened all the straps of my hands and feet.

But my eyes are still blindfolded.

(Translated by Siddique Mahmud)

VAILA SALINA LIZA

Date of Birth: 01 October

Place of Birth: Bangladesh

Education: Bachelor of Human Resources

Publication: 02

Lives in: New York, USA.

Email: lizasalina152@gmail.com

NOBODY LOVES YOU LIKE ME

Splitting the seclusion of the stone

The spring, that erupts, that's me.

Instead of diamond, I search to collect

Happiness among the stars

I stare and see

Our love has lost its sparkle there

O Loved One,

A bit of sunshine slips out from your body

And Fall on the ornaments of

Water-stars-light and sunshine

I looked at you and smiled again.

TAPESTRY PHOTOGRAPH AND MOMENTUM

I said I'll become a gypsy
Holding your hand
Desiring the silvery moonlight
We'll remain years after years.
Light-blue moon, lit the dreamy light
Or at the call of Ajan1
As-Salatu Khairum Mina-n Naum2
Touches the night and dawn
This is the only blessing.
And then the death-throe to love
and not to love,
And then the death-throe to love
and not to love.
Yesterday!!!?? It's enough time to forget
The antique you of long past.

AND AFTER THE SEPARATION

He has left yesterday from my life

That was a memorable day of my life

It's a straight story

Now I tell you

What I did yesterday,

With which I was busy yesterday

What is what, and what happened

Leave it, those are stories of yesterday

Those are only heart

Those are only Body

Only emotions

Only separation

So many yesterday went by

But my world remained the same.

I STARE AT YOUR FACE

The wind that touches your eyelids
Comes to me
The ant that roamed around your feet
Comes to me and say, how you keep
your steps, and where you stand.
As dusk descends, sometimes,
If I look at the sky, I can feel that
You've cast your eyes in the sky,

When you get hurt, instantly I can feel
Deep into my heart.

LET'S WALK TO THE PATH OF EXPANSE

1.

The age of distance between you

and me is lessening.

The settlings

Are composing the tunes on Tanpura

2.

You are erratic on the other side

The crows of cornices

I can hear you calling from this part

Still you and I remain assembled

And are not going elsewhere.

3.

I stare at you in specific way

Among a bunch of crowd

Both of those eyes get blind

But I feel the encouraging brightness in my heart

4.

Only you can open the eyes

Of my heart

To touch you

I feel pang in the furtive root of my heart

Come let's touch. I keep flying towards you.

OUR PREHISTORIC LOVE-WORSHIP

Distance gradually comes closer
Didn't you feel that I've been transforming
Into the radiating light of your body?

After compiling the history of the world
It'll be rational, if
Your and my biographies are not written at all.
Not countless, everything of us is accumulated
And turned into a unified life.
Rugged unseen life!

You've made your seat prepared by yourself
I'm sitting on the seat with enchanting
And then I make my own creation by myself
And I'll go on calling you Creator.

SLEEP, MY DEAR, SLEEP

When you're in sleep
I remain awake

Its evening in New York

The darkness of the night
In the canvas for my painting
Lights of your eyes
Are my colors.

I paint your sleeping figure
Only thinking about you
You remain lying dedicate sedating
I am touching your fingers
Those are my brushes

You are asleep
In my painting
I won't wake you up
I'll lie down a few moments now
Beside you

And then
Bit by bit
The meadow will fill up with grass.

I stare at you when I'm awake
And I see one million stars in the sky
Blinking beside the moon.

CARTOGRAPHY OF HEART

You can't understand
I search endlessly
You reside in my heart.

You told me
Not to stare at your exterior
But your inner beauty
Don't you understand
Whenever I stare at you
I could see inner and outer
Entire reflection.

[Translated by Siddique Mahmudur Rahman]

ABU SAYEED OBAIDULLAH

Date of Birth: 9 September 1965

Place of Birth: Kishorganj, Bangladesh

Education: Master of English Literature

Publication: 10

Lives in: Sydney, Australia.

Email: abusayeedobaidullah@gmail.com

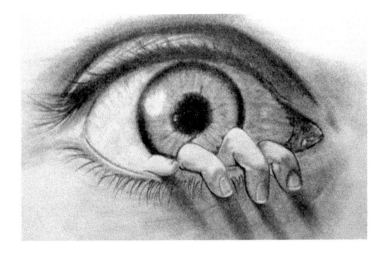

BABY FISH

From the bathroom, I smell fish fry.
Climbing by the roots, soap-foam in my chest
here are the eyes of fish, fins and golden net.
In front of me, plastic duck, wooden dog
looking for winter dwelling in the bathtub.

The soft, soft protein is blazing in the fire,
the forsaken, last javelin also making its way
through the tunnels of the fire.
And a baby fish is fast approaching through
the bloodshed and pieces of lips-
shredded beside the boats.

MIRROR

I'm watching my face in the much-used mirror,
the truth in the stories of evolutionist
is hanging in the monkey's tail of the zoo.
Stains of lost cities, settlements and fires are
in eyes and face. The glaciers and the arrow
of hunters are melting down the face.
You and I are walking after crossing
the No Mans Zone,
the que of children, bugle-horn of empty plates,
the wonderful time-game of the Earth,
envy of the history-
are all going down the hilly trucks like snakes.
If I were blind I would want coins, flickering of lights,
and the language of serpent from the Sun.
But now two eyes are filled with the
evolutionary blood!
Wars on lands, besieging, fall on
peoples' head like eagles.
The future of yours and mine
laugh with death sentence-
in the dust-laden mirror of the evening light.

NEAR THE SNOWY MOUNTAIN

Looking at the snowfalls,
I shall only recite poetry, I tell you.
The Sita- necklace at the bottom
of the White Mountain,
Dooldool horse, whatever comes airborne, I tell you.
Guards wearing red garments,
also show tricks and swiftness
of an alien country!

The ostrich and cats were about to go. The damsel,
getting out of the bus, has golden pigeon in her body.
I search frantically for wheat seeds.
Among all these unions of gathering,
man becomes tiger by grasping the breast of a woman.

The guests sat on the white grass.
Such a morning, at the breakfast table,
as if the human beings never boarded on the Earth!
Their memories of childhood are
identical to lithe wine.

We complete all our discussion after looking
at the route-knowing, wild solitary deer.

The path you keep cannot be fused with the snowfalls.
The shepherds of the black buffaloes-
shall go a far-reaching way, with the carriage.

INNOCENCE

I keep up my innocence,
dear mango tree you are my kin.
I attain your silhouette in this assembly of hunting,
as it is found in the perpetual mango-orchard.

Shunning propensity turned out to be a norm,
Still I sense ecstasy, still I long for love.
What do you send from the distance?
In the Bishkhali field, rifles of the enemy,
and pigeon hunting- these dazzling internment
as the hunters at wild.

In this overpowering wind
a single flicker also has a flowery flame.
With all mind and heart of innocence
I keep waiting and ignite the Agar-lamp.
I urge you to come, flying from
the bed of a flesh-trader and marry me.
Everything-- the long twisting necklace,
the cinema show-- are nothing but nonsense,
as is the idea of partition among the humans.

FARM HOUSE

Mind is joyful and communal in the farm. Archaeological fondness grows after watching the udder of the cow. A river-hypnotism in the foam of milk-ripples, the faces sink into the white maiden. The thrown away feather bears the Maya-seed and protein tree. Imagine, how a weaver bird teaches us the art of reproduction in the bush!

I get matted with you looking at the natural breeding act, and our future ideas float thinking of looming schooling. I write a letter, the language of clan in the morning of milking and art of extensive hand-machine. Thinking, how these hardworking cows teach us motherly convention- the dream-traveler of oxen.

PLASSEY

Ask. Horse O flying horse, who is
floating on your back?
Ask. If he is a reformer, traveler or a
secret messenger of the king.
Ask. Ask. Because there is an
assembly of people ahead.
Because we need to know, how many
houses will be burnt down
by the traveler!

Ask. Elephant O brilliant Elephant
how far will you go?
Or who will be taken with you? Ask.
Ask. As we have a dinner time ahead.
as we need to know which news will
sleuth the throat of young Khudiram.

The horse's coming and going
we have eternal layers of ice in the oven of villages.
The English are arriving, the Nawabs are departing
we have our graves, and skeleton of our forefathers.

By Pallasey we mean-

we have a sister begging from door to door,

with an empty plate of rice in her hands,

and the name of her unborn child is Siraj ud-Daulah.

A PATRIOTIC POEM

The water has turned into fire.
Today is the day when
one ignites fire on the bones
of traditions-loaded river Jamuna.

There is no boat.
We make fire by walking on the chest.
The deity of street is old-fashioned
he is just flying in the air by becoming
a half-memory,
that is also running fast
with the aroma of death.

In the great awakening day
the travelers sing songs,
oh, how the water of Jamuna has turned
into fire!
The fish-rice is blistered
along with the golden statues of dolls.
You live in the land of Gautam Buddha
and your life is full of ashes.

TO FISH

(Fisherman king at the bank of river)

Fish, I'm losing my patience. Sitting at the bank of the
river, oh fish, I lose my faith. You, neither coming out
of water- nor watching the beauty of the prayer. Fish,
fish I am dead. My boat has been destroyed; the black
Cobra has snatched away my fishing rod.

This night, my daughter is in puberty. Oh, fish show
yourself. The songs of rice are sung from country to
country, bones of people in the field! … fish you are
not coming out of water yet. The smoke in the
habitation, the moon is blazing--- fish, fish you still---
The puberty will be ended at dawn. We will become
barren, offspring less in the shrewd summer

Oh, fish you are not listening at all!

AT THE VAUCLUSE CEMETERY

The poetry of life at the cemetery
the Winter air is like innocent child-sleep,
chilly water's spilling out of the ocean.
The present and future cuddle people so easy!
I'm forgetful of collecting coins,
only the longing to play the guitar
quivers in the air and in the ceaseless grass.

The food lovers are shedding fats
from their guts in the fire,
the rows of Christ-tree on the cemented streets,
it does not seem one day they will rest in peace
like the friends of the graveyard.

How love and the words of affection
Are glowing like the gentle lights.
And the epitaph on the stones is
reminding that the commerce of the water-carrier
isn't everlasting!

WARFIELD

I've been left alone in the bloodstained blanket.
The border of barbed wires beside me,
how do I own you or steal you! I don't know.
The curse of land-besieging on my head
the enemy tents seem to be near and far
camouflaging rules over the nation
and traditions.

Everybody is vigilant too much
the mind is always tiger and tiger-like.
The mantra to occupy countries in my mouth
and the friendly rifles next to me,
the bombing airplane and the wounded
bird fly over me.

When will this crusade come to an end?
When will the javelin of Abu Sufian-
piercing the chest of Hamza
will be vanished?

Mother is waiting beside the barbed wires

The white flag is flown,
after the digging of tomb is finished.

SAD BONE

At the Balaka Cinema building
the new bridge reclines piercing
the Tagar flower.
shadow stepping down the Moon
can see the bench of his house.
Water is water and pitcher sitting together
in the hotel of the street.
Meghna and Jamuna change their
colours and flow through
the orange juice being poured
into the glass.

The shish kebab and Nan-bread
fur of wood-cat, monolith in every man.
Boys getting out of the bus
to smell the flesh of girls,
the electro wave runs in their penis!
Through frock trouser and odour in the armpit
whose weeding is today?

In the meantime

the echo of the canvasser ringing,

bringing the magic-evening

during the clash of roosters.

Water is leaf water

the vita-water of river Arial Khan.

When the fire becomes green after blazing,

the sad bone keeps awake

by splitting the Nan-bread into two.

AHMED MUSA

Date of Birth: 12 February 1957

Place of Birth: Narayanganj, Bangladesh

Education: Master of Arts

Publication: 24

Lives in: New York, USA

Email:

RHYMES OF FREEDOM

Meaning of freedom is legs without chains,

It's a ferry-boat without an anchor,

Freedom means a mouth without restriction,

Unadulterated ears, fearless heart,

Rahimuddin lives with John, Barua and Bishu,

A sovereign child on the lap of promising mother

From minuscule time to time eternal

Freedom is a unhampered flowing river.

UNIQUE OF ALL TIMES

It looks plain and simple
Sight fills with full of dreams
Head raised high, stepping bold
The entire village boasta about him
What's the mystery behind all this?
He was in the war in Seventy-One!
At times, many people turn into something else
But he is the hero of all times,
He is the courageous as he is Liberation Warrior.

INVENTED AUDACITY

You boast of being a courageous person
But now you are chanting in the parade against despots
Leave bragging, how big were you in early days
Now you're simply a doll, a cheap, of shameful metal

You know, you're a paltry worm, O you, tittle thing
Mokrom was in the heaven once,
Mussolini was very gentle at time,
All prostitutes were innocents.

It doesn't matter at all, It doesn't matter at all,
You home is in the pre-assigned darkest history.

TAIL STORY

Some people developed tails and a gorgeous tail
They satisfy others by waging their tails
Some people has gone too far, lost their senses,
They gurgle with honey, take bath with milk
They write poems with bayonets on human skins
Paints with bones, in undisclosed chamber.
And then, adore those poems and
paintings in gold frames
And satisfies the power-gods, making millions weep.

TO THE ESCAPISTS

If you want to avoid politics
You must have to cling to it
You may make fun of it from distant
'They are roaming around you all the times
Don't complain, and take up the helm by yourself
The country is there, and the country is your also.

Go ahead, O, you good ones, advance you valiant
The fiends will be cornered gradually
There are good and evils everywhere
It's not a new thing, very old conflict.

If you are good, the world will be good to you
If you are enlightened, spread the light to every place.

Taking hold of politics, Mussolini and Hilar
Has burned down the world into ashes
Churchill, Roosevelt, Stalin, or de Gaul
Are the sailors, are also the products of politics too.

A good deed of a good politician

Can eliminate the black spot of a century
Evil step of a wicked politician
Can throw millions of people into fire.

Whatever bad or good you get,
are the product of politics?
So, leave all the braggest and foppish shout
Throw them away, O, you, eliminate those all.

DOG AND MASTER DISCOUSE

The dog said to its master, 'I wag tails so much
But why don't I own houses and cars like them?'
Master said, 'It's your duty to wag your tail.
You do not have anything else to do at all
The dogs don't feel pleasure in
wagging tails, no life at all.

The dog grinned and unpleasantly asked,
'Then what's the use of being humans, my Lord?

FRIEND AND FOE OF RIVERS

There was a green village beside a river
One day it got a weird kind of disease
It wanted to embrace with the river Meghna
Now, the river devoured the village

The village said, Oh, You, A big savage!
You paid my offer of friendship,
by devouring dwelling houses
The river said, O you shut up, look and see
You'll turn into an island of soft silky sands
I'm pain now, but happiness at the end
This game of mine goes on all the times.

The river smiles mystifying and said,
I love you, so took you in me
Look at the white shoal on that side of my bank
The Kash jungle move like wings, new houses are there
Your dark soil shall be taken away by my waves
Day by day little by little shall be deposited there
You're dark now, will turn into white
You are but a big idiot.

You complain in vain, uselessly
Your dark face will be changed
I break down one bank and create another
If you are broken down, it's your benefit after all.'
In reply the village said, 'O my friend,
You shall flow on endlessly timeless
Why didn't you think, I too have some friends?
Farmers, weavers, potters and blacksmiths,
They'll lose their farms, crops, houses, too
Do you have any good news for them!
The river remained silent, couldn't reply,
The village knew, the river is silent,
due to lack of argument.

IT'S ABOUT WAR

War destroys people's life and property
Triumph and defeat consumes everything
Soldiers do not know why they fight
He obeys the order accurately
He has no right to question why
He has one job to perform, do or die

The heavy net of death is spread every where
The order-giver stays at safe and secured place.

TIME MACHINE

I'm unhappy for quite a few days
My time machine is out of order
I couldn't travel to past days
Riding the machine in the speed of light.

Journey towards future has also been stopped
I couldn't move on the light chariot happily
I couldn't move in the parallel world
Even couldn't eat death-winning fruits.

I can only enjoy that taste by reading history
 With that I add science fictions, I could feel a bit.

SONG OF WILD HORSE

Splitting the rope, holding me tight, ruining me,
O my wild horse, from one place do you take to other

Long time ago, one day I rode on your back
I destined to go to Neverland on your back
In which idea you galloped, I knew no target
O my wild horse, from one place do you take to other

You didn't let me stay in my home
Homeless gypsy, didn't you let me adapt
I probed for shade and body, game charm I played
O my wild horse, from one place do you take to other

i couldn't complete my eternal journey
Darkened death stood in front of me
If I can renew my life, I'll become your slave
O my wild horse, from one place do you take to other.

[Translated by Siddique Mahmudur Rahman]

RAVISANKAR MAITREE

Date of Birth: 16 December 1969

Place of Birth: Faridpur, Bangladesh

Education: Master of Bangla Literature

Publication: 53

Lives in: Ales, France.

Email: rsmaitree@gmail.com

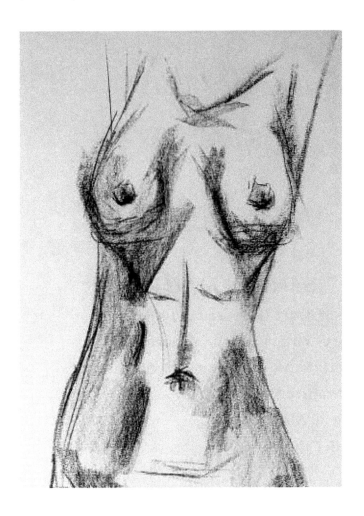

SWEET PLAY WITH GOD

1.

God is only manifested in human being. He takes the seat of human chariot. Man pulls the rope of the chariot. One must have an Ideal Guide to go ahead on the way to his supreme goal being led by Him. This journey starts at the very early hours of life and stops at the end. Meanwhile a very sweet play one enjoys with Him! And this is Life, this is worship.

2.

I cherished many good thoughts in me to make them implemented in action. But, my doing-urge as usual was waiting for a better moment to start. When the day ended; it started to get dark everywhere, I found nothing to be done at last. I got, good thinking comes to no work until they are applied in action. Success lies in proper action, not mere good thinking too.

3.

We can quench our thirst in many ways. Such as, going to stream, sea, and river or buying a bottle of water of a renowned brand. From wherever or however we do so, the only matter to quench our thirst is water. Likewise, the source of our spirit is only one. But, we also get shaped in many in this world. We play in different acts, but out of the stage we all are same human being.

4.

If you wish, give something to anybody with love and being egoless and not keeping any expectation in return so far as possible. Your open heart must be associated with your giving urge. To give is also worship. So it should be soothed with much pretty love and devotion. If you throw away a piece of loaf to any bird, you will find that it won't take it until you go aside; you stand far away from its fearing zone. Before giving, get ready for taking something politely. Look, an animal also feels no safety being close to you! Receiving something from someone with pure heart also makes one polite and this politeness helps one to give something with pure mind as well.

5.

When I was very little boy, I used to visit Paturiya village on foot. On the way to the village I had to cross a large field in the north, a river named Chandona. There was a Kali temple beside the road. It was very calm and quiet all around the temple and I felt very scared. At one time, I dared to enter the temple. As soon as I entered there I noticed that a priest was sitting before the goddess Kali idol. The room of the priest was just adjacent to the temple. His wife and children lived with him. Now I can recall that I asked the priest, "Don't you fear of this crimination ground?" In reply he said, "What fear! why? The fear of hunger is the main problem in this world and I'm very happy that this does not exist here."

- "Are you heartedly devoted to Kali?" I said.

He answered, "I am devoted to him who ensures my livelihood."

Since then, I would never fear of that crimination ground or goddess Kali as I walked through the road. I took Proshad (food offered to goddess) from the priest's hand. Why one should fear of him who ensures one's livelihood was my best and holiest teaching from that priest I had ever got.

6.

Everything is in heart, temple, mosque and church. He who exists in heart-shrine is God. But, we go to prayer house when we cannot find him anywhere else. We must get peace, even we get or not him in a prayer house. Rather we get the sweet accompany of the God-seekers. These accompany turns into organization when it is enriched and grown up; and organizational convention develops the civilization.

7.

When you sow a seed from other country, you cannot hope to have the same taste of the fruit the tree gives. For, the seed takes all the quality of the soil where you sow it. The work of the seed is to be turned into a plant. The work of being is being and becoming of life. Without this, all is regarded as ism. When ism gets distorted, it creates dispute among us. So, unless we can settle this dispute ourselves, until we can get rid of this problem, our existence also may be destroyed itself.

8.

As punishment compels us to abide by the laws so fear of death compels us to worship or pray to God. But it is a fact that we don't know when it will grasp us. Moreover, we firmly believe in afterlife and this is the main cause of keeping on so many rituals.

Similarly, one should not love his/her country being feared of punishment of law rather he/she should love the country to do something good for his/her country i.e. countrymen, and this love makes one a real patriot. On the contrary, they are real devotees who love the God without any reason being fully surrendered to Him heart and soul.

9.

I have come here not to preach, but tell something about the being and becoming of human being. I have nothing to impress or enforce someone to do what I say, but I have something to inform all. I don't want one to be adherent to me. Even, I wouldn't like to change or impede one's inborn instincts. I pray to God for the peace of all. I don't also believe in any worship apart from action.

10.

When I was in great distress, I had nothing of mine; I wandered here and there in deep frustration. My eyes were full of tears. I started to see everything blur. Nobody- even my relatives or friends was beside me. I couldn't see a single ray of light of hope. But, one day, in a fine charming afternoon, when I went out of my home, I got surprised! I felt a sudden thrilling in me with my all existence. I saw the whole nature turned into a great distinctive look. Everything around me was full of lives. I saw many blossomed plants all around with new green leaves. It seemed to me that all the leaves were just dancing with the tune of natural breeze. I felt a radical change in me. I returned my home and started to make a piece of land to be prepared for sowing seeds. Accordingly, I did everything what needed for having a good harvest. After some days, I saw my garden full of fresh flowers and even some vegetables too.

After a few weeks I harvested the crops and distributed some flowers and fruits to them who left me before alone. But, it's an interesting matter that they, then, offered me some more lands to make some more harvests for them. Then really, I didn't refuse their proposal. I agreed and tried to satisfy them heart and soul. At one point, they could realize that crops are more valuable than lands, and farmers are more than crops.

It's only then that I found myself to be a successful peasant, a successful human. Now all my relatives and friends know that nurturing our life is more important than our birth.

[Translated by Ripon Das]

SUBRATA AUGUSTINE GOMES

Date of Birth: 07 January 1965

Place of Birth: Dhaka, Bangladesh

Education: Master of English Literature

Publication:

Lives in: Sydney, Australia

Email: augustine.gomes@gmail.com

LUNATIC

The moon of Mars
Or it may be Jupiter's —
I'll never know what caused it to traverse
This part of the universe.

Yet it is moon, and because it is moon
I'll fix my eyes on it and hold
My paddle and my breath to soon
Row out of this earthen world.

FOG

The Golden Fog that one day
You stripped yourself in
Before the gaping eyes
Of Plotinus and Chaitanya
Has once more rubbed off the horizons, but
   Where are you now?

On Mount Sinai I sit
In a robe with your hundred and one
Pseudonyms written on it— but
   Where are you now
In such Golden Fog as this?

NOT A DOG IN SIGHT

The drawbridge opens and the red
Gap gapes with a lava river
Boiling beneath. I'm flying a Ferrari
Along Dusk Road. Progesterone
Burns in my fuel tank, but there's neither
A single speed breaker ahead nor a dog
Nor a marrow-harrowing howl of a werewolf...

The one that's sworn to subjugate me, my friend,
Will he be like… this gap— ever widening and
Red?

THE DIBBUK

Some clothes conceal
Some reveal...

I am your Dibbuk
      Or I am the pure you
I have digested you in my love
      And have become your you

Nowhere do I exist now
      Except in your being and thus
The container and the content have become one
      You and I us

Or we are only me
      Or you my misnomer
By me so thoroughly
      Conquered you are

CLOUDSCAPE

We are the busted and the blast

The alighted and the light

And yet the evening star and the morning star

We are— we are I and you and he and they

We'll sing a Charya now gashing our gushing veins

And we'll conjoin the two sides of the coin...

ALLEYWAYS

These alleys— that rip
Into rows of tall buildings
To vanish into some borderless dark—
Are your eyes.
I enter and exit these eyes of yours
Over and over again,
Mind-reader mine!

Whichever way I go
Unfailingly I arrive at some slaughter ground—
And you keep staring at me
From every corner of the sky,
Darkness incarnadine!

CONTAINING

I think I do it, but not quite;
It gets done of its own accord.
Yet my thought holds true— O lord!
How it makes me think!
Most cells have receptors, I was taught,
But a vessel doesn't contain if not set upright—
An upturned bucket does not hold a drop.
So some membranes are unfit for the job
And some, however scanty, are receptors not.

Which one is the stronger of the two?
Which one can drive me through this avenue?
The road has a road for its own sake
And another, for me to take.
Can it make me walk concurrently both?
Or can both of us travel the double-story road?
Ah! It makes me think!

A FORGOTTEN TUNE

Once upon a gloomy night
My only love had lost her sight
  And took me for a road
  And then, O heart! She rode
   Out of my life

My lamp blew out and I
Groped for her through the wood
Just as a blind man would
   On a gloomy monsoon night
   On a gloomy monsoon night

POISON

"No— No— No— this poison I will not drink!"
Same instant, same cry, mother and son together.
Who comes before, who after, who can tell for sure?
The son's extreme unction ere the mom's baptized?
Or the mother born with a dead son in her womb?

But we surely get by without knowing the full fact.
All that counts for us is that we have all been saved
Because they drank it; or are drinking it still;
Or because they will, because they doubtless will;
Ah, we've managed to turn a deaf ear to their cry.

THE GARDEN OF LOVE

This is where I stop, in the Garden of Love,
Amidst rows of upturned trees,
Where flowers bloom, like fireworks, underground —
At a siren's song the ripples on a stream
Are frozen in motion, luscious thighs still apart —
Lips would skid on glassy lips, if someone kissed —
And, in lead-melting sunlight, if for once I blinked,
Flapping its one thousand wings like a flock of gulls
The garden would flutter away into the convex sky —
Oh, how am I supposed to keep it still!

SALEM SULERI

Date of Birth: 27 August 1961

Place of Birth: Rangpur, Bangladesh.

Education: Master of Business Administration.

Publications: 21

Lives in: New York, USA.

Email: salemsuleri.ss@gmail.com

THIS WOULD BE THE
LAST DROP OF BLOOD

If you say this would be the last drop of Blood
The earth shall not stop the orchestra of weapon
Go back pincer civilization
Let's start war against war
Lament all the children of the World
Every day turns into a martyr's day
Prices of our tears are thrown away
By the armoured World to the dustbins.

We know
If you say this would be the last drop of Blood
Blood-coloured harvest will spring out
From the soil of Third World instead of green harvest.
Painful criminals will be hanged
Reporters will cover all the news of peace in vain
Popularity and prices of weapons will rise quickly
If you say this would be the last drop of blood
Diseases of women will be incurable infirm
In the soft areas of civilization
Children's of bombers will drop bloods regularly.

We live in the exquisite peace
Speaking the dialogue of poems
This conference, speeches and I am
A dreamer standing erect
Against blood bath, against weapons, against war
I inflate every day like a balloon of failure
I feel myself an institution working for peace
Or like an United Nations, because

However, we speak out that
this would be the last drop of blood
We again prepare ourselves for another peace talk.

A TALE OF TEST-TUBE RIVERS

Carrying water in pitcher have ended long time ago

Woman and man get tired of going to the flowing river
How long will they
open their portico, secrets of their body?
Rivers too are tired now
Where's raincoat, perplexed woman?
What unusual kind of cooperation
There's no youthfulness left as usual in the rivers
Not of itself, not of woman, nor of man.

There also remain unusual opposite journey
River is not a thing to observe
It now passes through tunnel
It is now felt with tube well, it is now supplies
Water to the houses of cities through pipes
Resembling snakes or bamboo
In the toilets, kitchen, gardens
In the summing tubs

Basins it flows as Test Tube Rivers

has now become fact

Water turns to human beings;

rivers are not in the rivers

Water flows towards water taps

O society, for you it is now.

LOVE IN INTERNET

Disk's love remains in the internet

Computer do not understand everything
CPU is but a statue
It's not a head of mind and brain
Disk's love remains in the risk.

In the living laptop
Love with a female developed through E-mail
At the end of browsing sweet dream develops
In both the eyes a building of plot is formed
Love in binary digit developed between the two
Filled monitor fills the field
Touching the mouse, I feel touch of the body
From CD Rom cinema inputs of multicolored memory
Everything is found through satellite network
Such beauty, such soft you are, only love-processor
But all ends with a click of shutdown button
But the main mistake is in preservation
If not saved the error turns to delete command
While pressing command to print

All efforts are lost, mind-button, touches the switch
Black eyes, floppy, virus, monitor is black

The entire memory dot becomes undone
 Disk's love remains in the risk.

TAKE THIS PROMISE OF FESTIVALS

Here, takes the golden happiness, promises of festivals
Purity of Autumn-dawn, white promise
Entire day, whole night, every moment
Only you remain awake.

Taking you as sky I throw my sight
Under the blue handkerchief cloud messengers
Comes down as lightening as the silver shield
Body tremble alone in the solitary night
Undress your naked emotion

Half white moon
Get drenched in the Sun's youthfulness, get wet
Tomorrow morning I'll be
reclining sun-rays on your body

Grab the latest news, dearest lips
Shall give monthly accounts with tuberose fragrance
Grab the comfort- labour
of two hundred and six bones of man

Take this your precious stone
of your heart, o dear artist
Take this golden happiness, promises of festivals.

THE PATH THAT BUILDS HUMAN BEING

'I've works to do' saying you stepped into the journe
Nostalgic dust flew high with the steps
Through the green field there's
parting line of woman hair
And meandering route of the river
Your conceited scarf flies like the sails of the boat flies

Once alone in the parting time,
maybe two months ago
You shed tears
Came back as the rubber cushion again and again
By the bush four eyes meet, fight of lips
Drenched youth poured down from the
cataract of heart
You can't go away saying I'm leaving many-a-times
'Look I don't like going, saying
When you neared
I termed that time as love.

'I've works to do' saying you stepped
crossing the garden

In the back recall of steps, open field, rural path,
greenery of grass

Far-away body goes far and both of my eyes

Finds suddenly grammar of path

Meandering rural road is not easy and straight

The path, that is built by men with their crooked mind

You too go away far today.

BLACK KISS ON WHITE EGG

Now-a-days good people lay fresh eggs,
And have a good night's sleep
And black people controls the market
By giving warmth to while egg by black feather
Hatches black generation
Cock- fight goes on with black eyes
Terrorist snap
They blacken the heart of white heart
On the alleys with their mane and dagger- eyes
Snatches away mental peace.

Black muffler, black weapon
Black money accumulates with these people
Livers of the capitalists are hostages under their nails
The black mask collects ransom in
exchange of the child.

Color of their blood is also red
But black sucrose intercourse in the flowers of heart
There's no boasting of yellow
The society is sacred of jaundice

And does on go out for sugar-cane juice
Bees gather at such place, black partners
Spreads black disease taking nutrition
Churns sins of bacteria and curse of the drain

Good people of distant lands never cast their eyes there
Getting love and good sleep, nice recreation
Lays fresh eggs, hatches good fetus
But good society is not allotted in the fate
Future generation runs after whiter country
That is an open naked free dark environment.

CULTIVATION OF CIVIL WAR

Two pictures on the wall - Memorable
We call one Scoundrel sometimes
God to the other,
Time changes,
Changes the light of the mirror.

Conciliation sparkles in one's face – as searchlight,
Darkness subsists in other, seems leader-bandit.

Once they were alive
The sun and the moon were there
They belonged in the days and night
Like others, these complete men survived,
neither they exploited, one another, 'The Worst'
Nor even in the tunes of these Dahook Birds.

But for lust and hate the successors
turned these pious souls
To crow and cuckoo
Bow down to search blessing from one
And throw away the other.

May be those pious and serene souls
Are sleeping in a single bed peacefully
Whereas we build separate dais- spread carpets,
Separate cushion, separate slogans- platforms,
Newer attempts develop cultivation of civil war.

CART-PULLER

Rest a while, wheel of misfortune
We will sing again after taking Bengali food
Again, we'll carry cause of
gunpowder, weighty constitution
We'll have to carry tarpaulin
of the stage of first May function
And take all the banners, festoons and
Dumb chairs and tables to the depot
Rest a-while bamboo-dais
Release those knots tied on the bosom
After a few times take up utensils, mattresses or
Suddenly in a deep dark night corpse of my brother
Lying flat face-down on the grass
Lost in oblivion the obituary news and closing news.

APRIL FOOL TO THE SUN

Waking up with the Sun in the morn,
With run and work,
After quarter of night, lie down to sleep.
Under this regulation
Human being found themselves tired, fatigued.

When sun is burning, youth is robust,
Deep is the desired Union,
But at office, labor-yards boiling people into work
In the male- less lonely noon's, bodies become stale.

I bade good bye to the sun
Whole-night the figures play waking on the bed
While the earth sleeps in the day, the sun confused.
May be pendulum developed cancer
May be the mistake of too old age.

Then at the evening-farewell
Our precious eyes full of dreams
We will tell the sub- April fool.
April fool to you.

Likewise, sun of muggers, moon of confusion
Carbon mono- oxide of politics, power chair
Let aside everything, come let's withdraw our names,
From voter's list and become cattle, goats or furniture.

From the stadium of mass killing, from United Nations
Peace Accord, from all embassies
let's withdraw humans!
All the red eyes that control the Earth;
that dictates all weapons
All the counterfeit bank-notes are the center of power.

On the contrary, the cowardice of humanity;
Without reversing, without walking the other way,
They love to lay.
Staying inside a shell, we let all know
Pedantic world, famous wild - this is your world
Keep it in rule or threat, you stay here.
 Humans won't reside here.
But the April fools ruling there.

DISEASE NAMED SNOBBERY

While watching deaths everyday
To think yourself immortal
It is a disease of cheerfulness
Maybe we can call it conceit.

What's its medicine?
Is its prescription, drug-list
remains in the Holy Scriptures?

Happy men turn stale
Says goodbye, my loving chair.
Leaves the seat with the speech
People are born in bunches
Only by one but never looks on
The journey of the ants, tiny deaths step by step …

All the months excitement procession touches
From heart to heart
Only the bridge of life remains.
Happy men behave like lunatic dressed like animals
Laughs with sunlight, sweats

in the night in intercourse

In good or bad names, feels happy in sweet melody
Most of the people seek for immortality.
Whereas at their feet ants goes on in rows
Goes on with procession of death
on their shoulders there might be coffins
So, snobbery I bury you, burn you down.

ZEBUNNESA JOTSNA

Date of Birth:

Place of Birth: Jessore, Bangladesh

Education: Master of Science

Lives in: New York, USA

Email: zebu.jotsna@gmail.com

FORBIDDEN LOVE

Have you come on the wings of Albatross?

In the snow-white region?

At the silent hours of night

Sounds of your footsteps and the smell of breath

Is shuddering the waves of wind

And is touching me

So thirsty eyes burn

Desiring annihilation.

AWAKE, O WOMEN

On the altar of beauty and devotion

Gaining the accolade of suave women

Even Goddess Durga sometimes becomes indignant

Not the favor of the prayer of women, he desires more

Women, rise with the

rapture of Creator and the creation

Not in the devotion of amour,

With the rumble of ocean and tumultuous days

Marveling episodes of Crisis-laden earth

Let drop down on the poems,

like the boiling Tidal boar

Flare up at the thunder O Woman, as a valiant warrior

Fierce claws of hyena and sword-sharp teeth

Open his character who comes to snatch away the
flowers of your body temple

Don't forgive him

In lewd eyes, grasping the chastity,

the dwellers of grave, crazy in your destruction

Burst! O woman, like a volcano,

Eliminate all incursions

Day and night the person burns you in the fire of insult

Live without him, who crush

your values and vend you negatively

Crush them all under your feet,

the entire universe

Rise like a Durga!

Annihilate all injustice,

deception that was made with you

O feeble! Silent woman, live once, for you only

it's your own Earth!

LOVE STORY

Have you woken up yet?
I'm waiting.
I want to look at you before looking at the sunlight
Your blemish face and messy hair
Are mingled with the dreams of the night
They also touched me last night with immense love
your lips have the touches of that felicity
I want to touch you before I touch the dew-drops
I want to drench my craving fingers
I want to feel, how many drops
of love have freezing on the lips
When you open your eyes, flowers will turn crimson
Bells will ring on my temple
On your touch, I'll float on the feathers of bird
With vinous intoxication, I'll sear, you'll burn too
On the waves of agonizing love
You'll speak out, O dream-wake,
have you come this morn?
How could I say,
for you T wrapped the sun in my body.

PARASITE LIFE

In silent secrecy, today we do not weave our dreams.

Like pigeons we don't discourse

under the whitish moonbeams

We do not exchange dialogue

Whole night in isolation, embracing,

We do not listen, cricket sing incessantly

Now we've become a bit of parasites

Parallel, reciprocal compromise

Like clever mushroom, we calculate,

We try to suck up each other

We pass our days as usual.

Let it be

Let the life only my own

Let the unruly seeds on the fast mooing wind

I smear sedentary waves of steam.

Mingling bits of tidbits on that

Why not bloom exquisite beautiful orchid

Let's fill the painless solitary time with

Artistic environment, then,

The meaning of life would be

Truly delightful.

DESIRE

If I were to get a new life,
Then I would be become a disciplined ant
As a queen on my own kingdom
I'd struggle, with my lover tenants
To yield future deposits
And lonesome me, walked
From one end of my empire to other
To look for you.

If I had a little more time
I'd fill the black and white canvas of the world
With multi-million colors
On the reluctant bank of the desired river.
Rectify all the errors
And become new once again
In the market of happiness-and sorrow
In exchange of painful cowry
I would try to acquire you for me.

If I could turn myself back
Then in the game of changes

I will make my fugitive heart feel
Nothing is lost in this world
They linger as it is where they remain.

The flower that bloom in the dry atmosphere
It has its life inside
Somewhere remain hidden.

BATHING IN THE OCEAN

I wanted to bath in the ocean
so, for a long time I didn't
touch the water of Shitolakkha,
I enchanted myself in nature,
I pass my hours in contemplation
The ocean is calling me secretly
In silence, the air has salty fragrance
The waves are soaking the sands, endlessly
What eternal power it has!
t smashes all my internal resistance
Like Shitallakkhya I too in immense expectation
Wait for that Eternal time.
Capacious waves, under the azure sky
Shall devastate the foamy destitute.

DISENCHANTED

Though it's too late
 Still I was at last disenchanted
I am free of worldliness!
Free of Humanity
Free of non-violence!

For years I saw the creators and the creation
 Has destructed Hiroshima, Syria-
splinters of bombs, the destitute wail,
The earth shudders. Humanity is gone astray
I ask, what's the suffering!
Is it for the Creator? Or the Creation?
I get no reply.
Therefore, revolting shout gradually
Comes out from the skull.
Let the pens are used as swords
 And slash down the disgrace of distorted savageness
At the extreme insult of humanity
I desire I could grasp the fire of wrath
into the clasp of nonviolence
And throw away with great

power into the Pacific Ocean

And then in great pain the fifth senses are disenchanted

In deaf, mute and blindness.

HALF HUMAN

In the slaughter-house of inhumanity
All the beauties of the world have terminated
The loveliness of moon-Sun, cloud and rain
Has clung into floating cruelty
of the poisonous ecology
The pointed reflection of the prism
Shows the animal-like developed half human
Clad in human dresses
These half humans ultimately shall destroy
The safe borders and gradually create
A peaceful and civilized unlivable dull earth.

THOSE EYES

Roses make me crazy
I'd still bow down before him
Who will pick up a sylvan-scented
Tiny flower from the grass that had just bloomed
On the earth and tell me, 'Look how beautiful it is!'
Enchanted by the silvery moon
On the shivery chilly night, I'll stay with him
Who will take me not to a dazzling dining tale
Of a five-star hotel,
But to a frosted lake, under the reflected Moon-light,
Kneel before me, shivering, and say,
"Look, another surprise of the world."

I want to look at those eyes, where
The fluffy clouds change color
The shredded leaves of the trees fly
And all the anguish
smile at the frankness of the children
And I'll wait with wonder for that evening
To see the world's most astounding sunset
in those vast blue eyes.

BLUE MOON

It felt as if I was waiting for you
For a thousand of years
O Blue moon!
Not a simple high tide
In your full moon gravitation
Flooded all my thirsty beach.
If not, like a violent boiling volcano
I'll scorch the entire world.

[Translated by Siddique Mahmudur Rahman]

ASHOKE KAR

Date of Birth: 2 January 1959

Place of Birth: Rajbari, Bangladesh

Education: Bachelor of Nursing

Lives in: Florida, USA

Email: tonmoy02@iCloud.com

RAIN ALL THROUGH THE NIGHT

Disobeying the rules are inherent habits of kinship.
Edictal blades cut into the soul, bleeding....
does it matter for life, for breath?
Inherited relations accumulate
as dust onto the dictionary of life.
Leaf's of the pine, listen restless wind,
Likes to settle down, touching your pleasant warmth.
It has too unresolved turmoil
of relationships squandered.
A lonely night dances around it,
Rain calls it through the night,
Everything widens openly, all over,
Still, the feelings for
warm-hearted leaves of Pine remain,

Too much affection is rained on forever,
Only the rain, that pounds through the night,
Draws alternate realities of relations for all.

HONEYMOON

Suppose, the sign of downfall was hidden into love,
with naive intuition we were playing around,
never noticed that the inevitability of consequences
was a smokescreen to reality? Our desires are far away,
carried by the wind to places unknown.

That's the way dreams are,
they take us to safe corners of the heart,
then, like gypsy tents, silently slip away....
Abstruse music notations,
are lost to the nimble musician's fingers.
To the unknown image
in the mirror, hiding uncontrolled lust,
only seen as the prism
is exposed to light, captured, but lost,

as fractured light, responding to
the heart's ghostly visions.
Suppose, the remaining pages of our history has made
tracks in the sands of time, with far-reaching shadows,
deaf to the noise of the wind, with a surprised fall

of rhythmic shapes, painted by a crestless moon.

Poisonous provocations were hidden

under affectionate greetings,

spreading into the air all around,

colors enjoying their fleeting honeymoon.

LOVE-BLINDED

With all the pleasant loneliness,
You brought three life giving red-roses,
During the time of shivering affections
Love pierced the imaginary throne.

Can roses too become poisonous instantly,
With unhindered inevitable blood drops in fingers,
As far as you are, being afraid echoes within me,
Piercing the darkness - holding light in hands -
Looking around to see wonders all over,
Lightyears seem not so far away at all,
Darkness around the light, the elegies of elegance,
Silently mingle into expelled petals of mourning,
Along with the fragrant heat of love,
Crystals get frozen onto the thrones of roses.

THE BIZARRELY FIRE

Look, what fire burns everything,
ravishing the life in its path.
Burnt clouds are fleeing away,
through horizons wanting them back,
birds with burnt wings drop down,
like falling autumn leaves,
burning of grasses are so pathetic,
it burns the inside deliberately.
What a fire,
so engulfing everything; inside and out...
The wedded desired to burn the self,
in a strange consuming fire -
think once before you burn yourself,
know, the bizarre fire, will devour all love,
burning yourself

And me too...

THE VOID

A void seems so strange to me,

drifting me ever far away

unbounded, I have never been

known of anything, nothing,

vacant of the heart,

all were unknown to me, but questions are;

How much do I know myself? Must

I expect a piece of the sky for my own?

May I realize those futile stanzas

are from my own poems?

The dusty smoke of forests burning the last of me...

Does lamenting really find life amidst Smokey timber

Sometimes familiarity can become strangers,

what illusory image is on cobalt glass,

Who are calling whom

by names unknown,

Does it for the mysterious self or for others?

Strangers, suddenly, may seem familiar, Is it really

Inside the illuminated

skyscraper window who's inhaling

exhausted breath,

that which implies a rule that instantly erases

self-recognition?

In front of the mirror, I try to recognize

unknown-myself, why I'm so unfamiliar to me.

Repealing shades after

shades of memories, I stand bloody,

old greetings seem modestly appreciating as a pleasant surprise, questions are spreading

strange unheard-unknown thoughts,

addressing prolonged applauses

Into the mystic mist; void seems so strange to me!

SURREALISM

Why the sighs are so long-winded
During the inappropriate time of the day,
With the luxury of dreams in silent verses.
When the day grows late, the night is awakened
By darker footsteps on the stairs,
A jingling of the key rings,
Following the gradually disappearing shadows
And the silent grotesque departure of everything
Me, since then I fade into the night,
And my long-winded sighs are embarrassed,
Are we so unfamiliar to one another?

That we fear the dawn's awakening.

EVE & APPLE

From inside my soul

The black cat jumped down silently,

Eve & Apple; black and darkness mingled completely.

Now, wherever

I extend my hands, there is a vast vineyard.

Now, whatever I want,

the red apple drops on my palm,

A pair of glowing cat's eyes,

Smoothly slices the darkness of the breakfast table,

Downstairs, footsteps bring a sea breeze with it,

On the breakfast table, we two

Harvest dreams and forbidden fruits.

IF YOU CATCH MY DRIFT

The world is beautiful, and yet,
filled up with cold people with gold coins!
Has the cold front from the Prairie?
I wonder, pierced their spine?
Watch carefully, you might notice
their bi-forked serpent tongues -
hibernating like reptiles
into narcissism's reflecting dreams.
When kisses of loved ones
turn ladies blue the crocodile's crusty spikes
get prominent rather than goose bumps!
These gifts have made lovers amphibious,
evolving into the missing links,
Yes, they are different, filling up the earth with
cold hearts, holding silver spoons between teeth.

THE HISTORY OF BIRTH

Suddenly at the doorsteps of existence,

Miracles are standing, with all its surprise,

In splits of a second, unfathomed emptiness abounds,

in front, in back.

Like the unknown Past,

The Future does not exist either,

The Present is the mysterious puzzle before me -

The only God Particles

Everything else has

disappeared instantly into the Blackhole

So, the Present is my only existence-? life and death-?

Something like a handful of savings,

The only tangible factors.

Rest of are only fantasies, illusions;

Languid forgotten dreams beyond the reality.

Prognosis, history of birth,

anniversaries, celebrating to celebrate

A billion light-years

spreading mysteriously into the universe

The birth of all nascent stars,

everything, all aspects, are the same as mine.
Just took birth with me,

At this moment,
Right now.

LIFE BEHIND SURREALISM

The Stoney moon stands watch over the mountain; dreamy moonlight has frozen the morning's mist. Scattered dreams are growing amongst the green roses. Light chasing the shade has almost reached the sky, drawing me besides you. Flying flocks of pigeons - searching for our dreams - a thirst for peace is scattered on the wind. Part of the sky, hanging on the open window, makes constellations seem so tangible. Here we are, hiding ourselves in the turmoil, with strange silences between us; under the vast water - like a tiny living species - like a drunken gambler, we play aquatics with fish and sea weeds, nourishing suicidal aspirations. We reach, absurdly, for compliments to one another. Into our loneliness we shelter, living seems so distant, dormant, waiting for the Spring. YOU become inevitable for existence to grow.

ABU ZUBIER

Date of birth: 4 May

Place of birth: Dhaka, Bangladesh

Publications :18

Education: Master of Business Administration

Lives in: Paris, France

email: emon4001@gmail.com

PERSUASION

Wide-bodied sunshine of the afternoon
Wants to know me,
Want to understand my evening story,
Want to know the declining damages,
Will the rays of light
Will refrain from kissing me?
Shall I enter the dense darkness?
I will be submerged into the abyss,
Am I still waiting to say these words
indefinitely still waiting,
Before the unnatural death of wide sun-shine
To me the mantra to live means illumination,
The light that drops down out of the sky,
To the wide sun-shine of the afternoon
My humble submission,
Do not deprive me at all
From the light of the blue sky.

EXPECTATION

I do not desire an unplanned death

An exact scheduled date of death is needed

So many work remain unfinished,

and if the death suddenly

There should be a policy on this matter,

After waiting for a long time

I got a date to meet my lover

And in the meantime, death soiled up everything!

A simple kiss was desired

I did not even get it.

Death should be put into discipline,

All the predetermined

works should have to be completed

And all persons should get a long life of a star

ASSISTANCE

You go on laughing, you go on singing,

You make me restless as your hair fly in the wind.

Make soak me in my heart

You burn out my time,

You become rainbow, sounding rain,

You become motivation with softening eyes

You like to remain hidden.

You feel the secret love.

You are the entire map of Padma

Some vultures surround you.

I send ocean currents

To protect you.

ETERNITY

The word I have uttered just now

Will that remain in the sea for eternity?

And will that blend in the ocean

Will that flow with the river,

Will that be firmly rooted in the mountains.

Will that be included in the United Nations document

Will that cause dust storm in the desert,

Will stop the war, or supply food

Will distribute humanity

Or will that end here,

or the word will be lost in the eternity.

IS LIFE FULL OF AMBITION

There are some expectations that are later found error
There are some desires which cannot be achieved.
The dilapidated desires ar ambitious
un-protective death news can easily
Be written down in the paper
Who struggle for others just a little
Who else decorate the earth for others
The life can be meaningless.
No, it can't be
Life the unstipulated.

COME HERE NOW

Still now I'm looking for a girl.

The girl might be even you

I have a plan

To start a new year.

I will bring change in my clothes, as you do.

I will smear my body with new perfume.

You will be fascinated,

My lips will be prepared for you.

I'll wake you up early in the morning

And I'll kiss you.

I'll swim on your dazzling beauty

I'm expecting you.

we'll not get any more time,

because there'll be Third World War.

FELANY

How many kilometers of land captured China,
The ice sheets of Ladakh, how is Naga Land, tell me,
the recent poet friend from Arunachal,
Is weaving industry in Manipur
is yet to emerge new flag?
How are you, Bangalee in Assam?
Hilsa of Padma does not go up stream any more
How many years Mizaram will sleep?
How the news will spread through
Thegamukh in moon light
Did the comrades of Tripura
forgot writing in Kakvarat,
West Bengal, O my West Bengal,
Whom is controlling Calcutta now,
Why the Jharkhand flares up,
Kashmir is now a death trap.
How many people died in Gujarat,
audacity kills human beings
Tamils do not know how to speak in Hindi,
When Punjab will be liberated
Jhelum, Chenab, Ravi, Sutlej, and Beas

How unknown is Bihar, Orissa do not know me?
I am Swadesh, my name is Freedom
Who prevents human beings by creating borders?
Shok-Hun-Pathan-Mughal disappeared,
Memories fade away, people are lost,
But Felani, you are the symbol
of India in decided partition,
Russia is now in my memory now
The nuclear crisis entwined in your body
More furious than thousands of volcanic eruptions
Brightly illuminated than million suns
 Which is this light, that make my body lacerated?
What is this fiery deluge, if it touches the cold body
The body breathes its last?
Ask the hungry people today
Ask the hungry state.

I THOUGHT

I thought I should protest alone

I would leap alone in this fight

I thought I would take leave from the office,

Shall go to the mountain and see the sky,

I'll investigate the constellation

I thought I will build up a huge asset,

I thought, I will be a human

being, shall show violent attitude,

I thought I will become an warrior, I will liberate

The northern mountain lands

I thought I will poet

I will write poetry for hunger strike,

I thought many things more

Some thoughts are of faraway,

some closer thoughts get annoyed

And losses in never-land.

BOUNDED BY THE SKY

You've bounded the frontier of my flight by the river
You've set the boundary of the swimming by the ocean
You've set the hill to limit the route of the ship
You've restricted the height to see you with the night
You've fastened my world of light with the morning
You've closed the vision of moon light by the sun
You've stopped the emptiness by the flights of crickets
You've obstructed the dew-drenched wet green field
If you are taken away, then how could I get you
I am obstruction, I'll now
be Krishna and you are Radha.

GRISLINESS

Is the colour of time grey?
The location changes sideways
What is the colour? Conflict?
The colour of coral oozed from the green moss
Moved away from the side of life
I am moving away from its side
I do not if sky is the time?
What can be the color of the time in the sky
Moved away from the moss
I rise from the coral-drenched water
I'm sweating in chilly water.
I control my cold with my sweaty nose
Now, as if the gray time. Time is passing
I do not know in reaction today I am turning gray
I do not know if the time is gray.

[Translated by Siddique Mahmudur Rahman]

FERDOUS NAHAR

Date of Birth: 4 October 1962

Place of Birth: Dhaka, Bangladesh

Education: Masters Degree

Publication: 18

Lives in: Toronto, Canada

Email: ferdousnahar@gmail.com

HEART MUSEUM

I was never born
I walk amidst the subterranean
darkness digging in the birth and death
I have already learnt that
I will never be born in this turbulent human world
Roaming among museums of the world I have
come across lots of archeological exhibits

The fragmented sighs blended with seized memories
There are so many museums and
I am searching for their secret doors
Where tunnels have been built reaching
towards private balconies
The heart has flown to the untamed rocky summit,
The horizon has reached the bone lanterns
Small and big, empty and full,
void and hollow, myriads of hearts

Gather in the casket adorned with sighs,
deception and much more
And wait for ages in silence within a session.

I will never be born to witness this,

Now a fierce shriek is carrying me away

in a flying saucer

Today a new museum will be inaugurated…

THAT WINTER

I can't remember where I have lost those letters
I have tried heart and soul to remember,
where could they be?
I go around and round from the
bookshelf to the almirah.
But I can't find them, they are nowhere,
they weren't supposed to be lost though.

I spent a long time in the rain sanatorium,
it's just today I have been discharged
The rain sanatorium! The numerous chemo
therapy of jingles, rainstorm!
The diffusion of the singing rain within
the harmony of psyche and brain!

That Winter he gave me to read
Siddhartha by Hermann Hesse.

THE FUGITIVE LOVER

I have just completed treatment for my ailment.

I am given the diet of an entire sky,

a sea of disaster syrup.

I don't like taking them all by myself,

so, I invite the passersby.

I call out, hey! come and drink the fluid of life,

Come, swallow a couple of tablets

Let's share and be oblivious of all the life sentences...

Rust has formed on the iron gate of distant dreams

Now echoes precede the sounds.

The age-old darkness finds relief when

the new star doesn't rise in the sky.

My doctor is a popular fugitive lover

His leg is tattooed with the image of self-torture
through millions of years.

He happens to be the next door neighbour of Zeus.

Zeus had seduced his lover

Although this is not inscribed in the

mythology, yet everyone knew it

Since then my doctor has been prescribing arid river...

I am his persistent patient, since he knows
me for a very angry person
Every day he prescribes me numerous
high tides and low tides.

THE EMAILS ARE ON THE BERLIN WALL

Hey, have you all forgotten me?

I send you so many Emails, no reply,

then suddenly I ponder

While the astronaut minds

of humans are so eager to forget

Would you be different?

I decide to forget

Those who have forgotten me,

Even the one, who told me once,

all my moments mean you.

No moment has ever been born without

you being there.

Now he is laughing and calling me a spy,

and telling me,

You cross the Berlin Wall in the dark

ignoring the fear of getting shot at...!

You seem to me a terrible person, you know?

Will you please excuse me, I need a break!

Tell me, how can I blame you?

The sound weapon is breaking everything all around

And business is attacking people's waggly wonders!
Now the wall is being sold in tiny pieces
In the world market, I also have
some in my possession...

All my Emails are roaming in
bewilderment around the Berlin wall.

SLIGHTLY CASUAL SLIGHTLY FORMAL

I want to die for some days
I want to sleep without breathing for
some days in an uneven dark room
Please forget it, and never mind, this is
The latest addition

Even when life dries up, on the other
side of it the flowing river speeds away
Everyday leaving a handful of stories
of the goldfish like a fairytale
Therefore, I am angling in the dry
lake and hold on to the line with a hope
Lest my catch happens to be an enchanted memoir

The maple leaves are drowning in the water...
whenever I look at the scene, the innate demon
From my mind glares at me and reproaches,
Go home and find out how much more is
Drowning every day, do you have any idea?

Whenever I close my eyes, I see a lone pregnant train rushing through the impenetrable fog…

I rush gasping with labour pain and find the station overcast with torrential rain,

The lunar month passes, the citrus smelling

mind floats away

Only the desolate fog knows the

opinions of others about kissing.

DWELLING IN THE POST OFFICE

I had a desire to dwell in the post office

And float from cities to cities sticking

stamps on my forehead,

It never happened, so

I sit and wait here at the frozen dockyard

Ignoring the gnawing of extreme wintry weather

I crossed an unworldly moonlit meadow

Reaching towards a worldly city.

I beheld with my own eyes

The enormous moon changing clothes over the

enormous meadow,

I sketched it with delicately chosen words

and posted it spending the highest postage…

The bird and the telegram fell asleep

together inside the envelope!

The dancing dockyard shook on the

waves and skeptically retorted,

"You will accomplish nothing in life!"

Even if it's nothing, isn't that still something…

THE ARTWORK OF THE FRENZIED WIND

Across the river of sighs our little shack waits

There the frenzied wind creates intricate artwork

all day long

Where to stand so that

the colourful brushwork will not get smudged?

By which fond name to call to hear

the fond reply, this is what I like?

The fidgety gallinule sings all day long

The picture panorama of nature

allures as it unfolds the beauty

The morning is knocking on the door along with the profound amour of sleepless nights

The bustling clouds imbibe the time unknown

Yesterday while my knee was bleeding a pang besieged me all day long, feeling dejected I paced fast leaving behind a trail of blood drops... as I have painted an artwork with them, quite unknowingly I watch from a distance how the brushwork of blood is getting wiped off under the swirling steps of the sufee dance, how the veiled secret of the quick-sand is getting washed away while the waiting shack swings in the distrait wind.

IN THE BEGINNING AND END OF POETRY

A photo was posted in the beginning of my poems
An empty rail station, a blue train,
a pregnant woman and a man behind her
I had no idea what was in the editor's
mind behind selecting this photo, but I liked it

There was a tree on the red
soil of the foggy rail station,
Around the tree was a pedestal
in blue and white, the green twigs, closely entangled
The close-knit leaves
were cuddling each other and shading the sun
While swinging on either side of the station,
From the station master's room,
one can see the faraway road, rail crossing
A stopped train, people getting off and on the train
The train moving slowly and going away,
afterwards a dense quietness…

The pregnant woman walks alone,
someone walking behind her

I can't guess what time of the day it is
It could either be noontime or on no time at all
The woman walks along, the baby
in her womb moves and looks
A cat mews around….
The station asks the baby to sleep,
the baby tells the woman-

Don't stop mom, keep walking!

SOMEONE SLEEPING ON THE SAND BED

The last time when I saw him,
A shining river gave me
the pillow and blanket and told me,
You can go to sleep now.... go,
cover yourself with the thin sandy blanket and sleep.
Since then I went to sleep. As I sink in the strange
rhythm of the desolate river breeze,
Every time I turn on my side
I feel like I have someone close by.
Despite knowing that
the river does not like it, he sits and stares at me...
The river insists on him to
let me alone and let me sleep
'Can't you see how she is drowning under land and
water, in the slush? Please leave her alone!
Perhaps you could come back after she wakes up and
stare as long as you want!'
I thought he would understand, and I would be able to
have a long sleep on the sand bed.
But he doesn't go away,
I don't think he will. I can't have a sound sleep.
Someone waits in my sleep on the sand bed
The river flows away...

TOO CLOSE AND TOO
FAR AWAY FROM ATHENS

I had no vision, so you called me blind easily!

A storm evoked when I walked
on the archeological plain
Hand in hand with Homer! The fragmented history
Shivered wrapped around the hands of the epic…
Both of us were without vision…
While we kissed with sizzling
passion amidst pin drop silence,
The wall paintings ushered
in the mellowing saxophone.
A troop of born-blind sailors
were swimming in the age of water
Valets were waiting with
the dress at the bathing-house
The band was playing
hydraulus in the half lit half dark yard,
The singing raindrops embraced the bathers…
We stood under the quiet acropolis shade
Diffusing ourselves into the ruins of temples

Or the ancient tales of the golden era.

Our village was immersed under the ancient rain
In search of a little bit of warmth, as if too close
Yet too far away from Athens,
like the unresolved hydraulic riddle,
Echoes from the dark
era remained like blindness incarnated…

[Translated by Lubna Yasmeen]

MOHAMMAD NASIRULLAH

Date of Birth:

Born in: Dhaka, Bangladesh

Education: Master of English Literature

Lives in: New York, USA

Email:

INTRODUCTION

I should tell about yourself who you are
Before I introduce myself who I am
I should tell about yourself who you are
Before I introduce myself who I am
You are a Dr. of Philosophy
I believe you are a Dr. of Law
You are a great architect
You are creative, a design artist
You are a master of hearts
You are an MH.

My name is Muhammad
The other name is Hula
Middle name is Nasir
Last name is Ullah.

I blog my poems
In "not you dot us"
I am not you
Like you are not me,
 We are together us.

Dot looks like planet
So, US look like universe
Bangladesh is my Desh
You are the best.

MHEICH

Who programmed us
A stupid application
Who made us
A stupid application
Who is the stupid developer?
Who made us
A stupid application
Who was the applicant
A stupid application
It's the immigration
Visa application.

We the system hang
In the middle of action
We the system crashhhh
In the middle of action

We got fixed
After crucifixion
We the system get repaired
When dead or get retarded.

We the system suffered

The lack of truthfulness

We the system suffered

The lack of skillfulness

We run short

When you kick

The power button tick.

We are computers

 Oh god Human avatar

We are not so

Stupid application.

We are here

To give a better vision

We will be there

With record of every action.

A DROP OF RAIN

Every word the man says
Every word saves
Every word gains
The Spiritual rains.

THE FRUIT OF MELANCHOLY

My songs sing
  Love me as much as lovers are doing
  See
  When I be your own
  See
  When I am laying down
  On the ground under the tree
  or
  I will be somewhere
  Wandering alone
  You will be None
  Knowing me lonely
  Fruit of melancholy.

GOOD

You say I am Good

Enough for you

Because I know certain conditions

Fit you to go

Where I want to go

With you Mo

I know that rules

Which make the lawww

And under the lawww

We all shall growww.

SYMPATHYYY

I will keep holding thinggg that is
Too much for you please,
But you need to go slowww.

Go from there
Remember the parable of crowww
Get the ropes n' climb the tree
And bring the fruit
And place it before meee;
Then I will knowww
About your sympathyyy,
And then
You will get the thingggs
For which
You are dying fooor.

OMG

My god you are so unlimited,
You are so Unlimited oh my god.

There was a big nothing
Before you appear as Unlimited
That's why nothing happened
Until this moment
Happy Birth Day
My Goodness!
Happy Birth Day Dear
My God!

Who was my god before?
A big nothing.
Now it is Unlimited.
My god is unlimited,
Unlimited is my god.

From the beginning,
It's unlimited
from the beginning

Till the end
It is unlimited
In all end.

Beginning or ending
Ending or beginning
All is the same.
My god is unlimited
Unlimited is my god.
She is alive
And she is not dead.

UDAY SHANAKAR DURJAY

Date of Birth: 05 January 1981

Place of Birth: Jessore, Bangladesh

Education: Master of Science

Publication: 01

Lives in: London, UK

Email: usdurjay@gmail.com

UPROOTED!

As the banks of Padma and Buriganga occupied
Stacks of files, who supposed to question for their land
became penniless from their Jamindari.

Uprooted!

As the map became occupied,
When the pride... honour of a girl became non-existent,
When there was no such value of human rights
for the sake of oppression

We got uprooted and some others celebrated!

All the addresses, temples
which were belonging to others

got occupied and we became
penniless and stamped as Refugees.

Shelter camps became the single option
as we got uprooted.

But, conscience?
The pens of those brave
hearted children, whose parents
fought for their freedom are still working as triggers.
As the emotions and the tears
Can't be uprooted
Can't be occupied.

ESCAPE TO SURVIVE

An amoebiotic extremism became the reality of today.
People are destroying millions of lives and assets
for the sake of religion.
Seems like a medieval barbarism
where people are still scared about religion, vengeance,
splashed blood, terrified sleepless nights.

Now only silence finds
all the way to a gloomy weather.

As the neighbours destroy
the faith, demolish the households,
the lamps which were supposed to be lit every evening
the honour of female
inhabitant, buried by their neighbours.

We earned our heroic freedom in 1971
Again, we lost our relatives
in 1991 where extremism met the first priority.
We had only one thing to think about...
Escape to survive!

We watched the terrifying,
barbaric Babri Mosque and Rama Temple massacre
We fought in 2001 but
were unable to achieve justice for our relatives
We became marked
as Malaun, not as a normal human being.

A Malaun! The identity
which was given by our neighbours.
Now, as the Vengeance,
Prejudice and evil manners became
the daily sequence in our society,
Only the survivors become winners.
Escape to survive Sudhangshu!!!

NO ONE WRITES A POEM FOR A FATHER

(To Professor Ajoy Roy father of Dr. Avijit Roy)

Being suffered by the deepest
pain from millions of years
When poets write their feelings, which express
the extremism of the homeland,
will remain a silent viewer
of the saddest part of the story.

Ajoy Roy, had to face the situation,
A father, who was not so blessed,
Had to carry his son's dead body,
had to collect the scattered flesh

Of his daughter who
was supposed to be the most unwanted

Blood stains still can
be found on the road sides, at the book fair
But it's only the soul
of his child which makes a father more than the God.

Tears turn into molecules...
Have we ever thought
why does poetry not denote fathers?

Why fathers like Ajoy Roy suffer terribly!

A GLOOMY CORNEA

A gloomy thousand
square miles turn into pin drop silence
when a father carries
his child's dead body on his shoulder.

Tears becomes obvious and the ultimate
When a father had no other address to ask for help
When a father feels like distressed sailor in a mid-sea

Finding his belongings
all the way to Nordic moonlight.

O dear papa!
You the man, who
has enormous courage to bear the pain
The situation left you on a battlefield alone
Where millions of blood shots
only can protest their grudge

Where thousands of missiles
are stacked ready to deploy

Where Darwin is still waiting
to such species of a father.
Only a strong glassy defensive
wall is there to protect the father

Dreams are speechless, as
they have no words for condolence

Father is fighting alone...

SONGS OF INNOCENCE

Writing those sleepless terrified nights where a life
just ended for the sake of religion.
Penning my feelings on blood scattered maps which
still can be found on Charlie Hebdos's table.
I try to write down the pain of 3.7 million
souls on the road sides of Paris.
Still penning down those memories of Dhaka where
We encountered the dark
smoke of petrol in fresh oxygen
Witnessed the massive
change of society, living in a sudden
Only bullets have the word today
Burn units became the home of Innocence,
youth and morning mocking birds
All have changed their way of life.

My homeland is still burning.

EXPECTATIONS OF A BRIGHTER MORNING

Nur Hossain will beg pardon in front of millions.
He will be back again to stand for those seven families
which were affected by his past.
Osmans' also turn down their greed and cruelty
and come back again into mass. That day they will
also try to adopt those silent words of Twaki's father.
When those Hajari stops their death toll
and accept us as their brothers...
We will work together to build the Bangladesh.
A new sunshine will be visible when
the roads of Fenni will
turn again a peaceful part of love.

HEARTBEATS OF MELANCHOLY

Down memory lane I wrote all those instances
on the mythology pages of the life…
where strains of water
creates the ornaments.
Wrote down melancholy of rivers
where a dead nightingale writes
about little girl's daily diaries.

Wrote down about those
dusty roads where we left our childhoods
Clouds still float like fountains
but roads are not same as before.

I am still writing about those days where

Heartbeats turned into melancholy.

WHEN GENERATION CHANGES WITH PEN

Life has been changed a lot
Focusing the achievements in a dusty pale
Nation is still facing hard days
Children of those freedom fighters who fought
For their homeland; become looser like those
Sleepless birds.
The Prabeer Sikdaars defeated in 1971 and still they are
keep loosing. But still a dream of a better tomorrow
In Faridpur and a deep pain to see the protest
march being stopped by the Rich
Today,
Sikdaars are by the roadside to survive. All the
disguisers have changed,
Religion becomes their weapon
as they have taken a new oath to fight
They are fearless, they
are cruel but still they are the one who
help to rule!

ANTHEM OF TOGETHERNESS

We never expected such a gloomy moonlit night!
You promised us a brighter sunny morning where
Everyone will sign the anthem of togetherness
Where no one will stop a boy when he waves a flag !
Where in the evening Bhairabi songs
will be sung near Keertankhola
Wounds will be removed from the dead bodies.
Azad will return during the fall
All the bullets will have no excuse to burn
on the cornea of a wild pigs
When pigeons will come
again, on the 32 Dhanmondi's lawn.
You dreamt of demolishing
the negativities of the society
Jaynul Abedin's portrait of poverty will be sold out
Where Goon will write
the second part of Premangshu's blood.
Where Rahman will write glamorous
poetries again...
But...
We never expected a gloomy moonlit night.

AN ENDLESS VOYAGE

You are my fresh eyes of monsoon
You are my sunny afternoon
You are the wintery pacific
You are the excitements of lazy noon.
You've made a new dimension in morning mist
Uncertainty in the busy streets,
An endless voyage in hard days.

You are a sudden diluvium of moonlight
When you unconsciously take the shower of
Morning sunshine, my anticipated eyes
Seeks for leisure with you.

MUJIB EROM

Date of Birth: 21 October 1969

Place of Birth: Moulvi Bazar, Bangladesh

Education: Master of Bangla Literature

Publication: 26

Lives in: Birmingham, UK

Email: mujiberom@hotmail.com

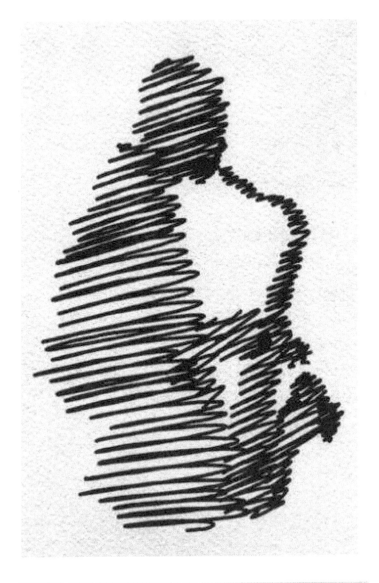

MY VILLAGE NALIHURI

If called by own name, vanity of fathomless road shatters. Whatever by birth…whatever is Nalihuri…whatever own name…own land…self-discipline…up rises the din and bustle of my own.

People walk only in bounded water. Although some of them walk up to distant Greece. They travel even further and return learning the age of old tree. The vast water body of Lake Amazon! Afterwards, even if someone falls asleep while taking rest for a while beside the strawberry plantation, at that very moment someone would call him by his personal name.

People just forgets his own place, own verse. Then he roams around the five great rivers – and discovers his true self by the dictation of natural laws. Today, in the morning, Erom realized this great truth of life!

BEARING LETTER

Tell me who else will send a bearing letter to your address?

In Aloi'sshop, does one still gets those 'forget me not' printed pages? So colourful pages, how could I send such a nascent heart?

Does your name still ring in Kamalpur? The postman who records the waves of his works in quickness – does he know that your handwriting suddenly sparkles at dawn?

Time looms over at the post-office. Does that ornament design-book in the jewelry shop still accumulate time over its pages? So many designs, so much golden sandal spread, why did I spend the day in the jewelry shop waiting for the mail?

Waiting in the queue – hey postman, please call my name at least once, say the address, say a bearing letter has arrived! While paying the postal duties I take out from my pocket a couple of deer!

N. B. : He who used to make exquisite covers of your books tearing the Soviet magazines – why his books are now falling, torn apart!

WHAT OTHER THINGS HAPPENED TO ME BEFORE VISITING THIS VILLAGE

Dusk sets in the centurion lawn. The soft breeze returning from the lake makes the evening more charming. The eternal trees are putting on the pulse of sundown laughter. Still the chirpings of so many birds have been left over. Seems this evening is not an evening I used to know; it is undressing its lighted gown on the bank of thousand-year-old river. Mesmerized I listen to the chirping of the birds. The murmurs of the leaves. What a din and bustle on the branches! As if I used to live here, with these flowers, leaves and birds, for centuries. I have fallen in love with such an amazing twilight; had a very intimate conversation. I was young and I had profound love for someone.

Now the homebound birds evoke memories. This me who is now traveling far, owing to a wrong mood, those home-bound birds don't know the deep cry of this heart. Such a gentle evening, the birds, the leaves, the wind, and the flowers deepen the setting! Makes me utterly disheveled!

WHAT I JOT DOWN FIRST IN MY DIARY AFTER COMING TO THIS VILLAGE

You provided me a blank page! An uncultivated land! Tell me, what crops I should grow on that virgin terrain! I am the son of farmer, leaving behind my parental profession, I came to this strange hemisphere. Though I want to capture some words in the sowing season – I have less power, I only have adoration for disposition. Once I left my village and came to the town, that self of mine landed in the domain of capital following your sentiments – my ill luck forces me to do some cultivation of words. In the blank sheet given by you I build an abode of passion.

THE TRUE AND ORIGINAL POEM

Why adoration stays outside

Call it in

The noon has rolled over verdant pasture…

It's better to abscond this poem here by leaving some blank space rather than continue writing the way drawn above. At least some needlework has been created! I keep it aside for some unknown place. I know it will also learn how to call someone with the wink of an eye. I become a traveler among the travelers.

Over a thousand years I may be writing – forget me not…

MY GARDEN

I desire the flower of a hedge-plant!

Gardens, which still remain on this Earth being concealed by bamboo spikes, the teenage girl, who still, keeping aside her textbook of higher mathematics, opens the window to read the fragrance of sweet-scented flowers, I sympathize with them.

I am not an admirer of such house on whose lawn Jarul flowers bloom keeping a suitable girl unloved. Rather I desire the quay of a quite pond surrounded by the shadows of rain-trees.

CULTIVATION

By mistake this page has remained blank.

By mistake and by laziness countless white-pages have piled on my life. I haven't planted any fruit-bearing tree on those virgin lands. Finding them empty, weeds have grown by large on them. Haven't a wild flower grown and bloom amidst the weeds silently, secretly?

I also ponder over that.

I consider leaving some spaces untilled isn't, as such, very bad. Sometimes flowers bloom on them by chance, quite silently, beyond our sight.

VANITY

The vanity that has caused the harm. Oh, call him. Give him the low stand to seat. Entertain him like an honored guest. Dance with him in the flowering forest of honey. Then you will see the vanity is under your control. Now give him the sensation of tickling. Keep him long as a fresh fish in the earthen pot. He is Lord Sri Krishna! The pride that has brought destruction.

Pondering Mujib Erom says – it is him who has quenched the fire. The self-esteem that has caused the damage.

NEIGHBOUR

When you chase a dark-brown coloured calf dancing down this ridge of earth between black cumin fields, I collect the grass-flowers of your route. Our ducks always swarm your pond. Your stocky rooster keeps dominating our aged lawn. Our milk-white hen frequently disappears in your shrubbery. Sometimes I give the dark-brown coloured calf a bath and ponder – would you come to this cemented moorage to take a bath! The lights of your portico keep illuminating our path. I return home whistling. I swear, you are the wind of my return journey, with which I fill my bosom!

MY VILLAGE NALIHURI [2]

The Second Excerpt extracted from the Original Book

Let me tell you at the outset, believe me, whatever I have composed, so far, have been printed in my birthplace in some or other form.

This home where I reside now is a transitory dwelling, for God's sake, trust me, has been printed on my figure by sheer chance. I keep memorizing only one name, whose immense glory I describe!

Whether you believe or not, Erom has not traveled anywhere, at any period of time, leaving his village – Nalihuri.

[Translated by Kamrul Hasan]

MAZNU SHAH

Date of Birth: 26 March 1970

Place of Birth: Gaibandha, Bangladesh

Education: Master of Philosophy

Publication: 07

Lives in: Brescia, Italy.

Email: maznushah@gmail.com

EXPRESSIONS

My verses are born in the silence where Zebras play
with their colts. After a long expedition, I've found
a page marker, an intense negation and the shadow
of a dazzling pomegranate. Gazing at the shattered
clock, I start to write. One side, my oceanography
classes and on the other side, my desire of swimming
with you. As I enter this house of cards, you
always ask whether I am a Libra? Are you Kanonbala –
I ask her in reply. The conundrums are now at its best.
Your aroma is just like grasses.
Here I open the window;
and see vendors coming back from the marketplace,
bruised & battered. Starlight pours into our house of
cards endlessly.

[Translated by Andaleeb]

SILVER-TONGUED GODDESS

I have never seen such rumbling clouds, let us talk
about hara-kiri; or you want to
define some cosmology?
Here come the hermaphrodites! Let us now talk about
the sadness of the crotons. Desire,
beauty and sin; walk together.

Don't be so shy my silver-tongued goddess, don't ever
look at the bitter-moon. The curse-flower has finally
bloomed; I'm so lost in it. Just be a little blithe; she is
with an endless cricket-hymn,
she is with a thousand of
pointed needle onto her face. Isn't she a weedoholic,
a desperate night killer – just like you?
The lexicon of mutes is lost in the maze of tamarisk.
Now I'm sleepy; let
the old musket be my pillow. I came
here to clasp your harvest in the name of the holy King.
I don't have talents; so, I used to follow the tweets of
yellow birds, and the narrow trail that headed to your
hexagonal granary.

[Translated by Andaleeb]

ON THE RED HILL

One day the Moon itself
will creep into your bedroom. Then you'd think
who's gonna get those cloves and
cardamoms. Here you can roll back your
grass-carpet. Text has been
long dead, so do the spice charmer, and every
blade of the golden grass. We can't
foster a thing here; neither the brew-star
nor the wind-chime; a kiss, or just
a gas-lamp! Here I must stand right
before a sage tree; or jump over
the Koka-Shastra and the fatal cracks. In
the slant of the Red Hill, I
met the cloud-mistress. She left the cluster of
keys as I flipped some
magic-circles. Hasn't she come here to teach me?
Oh God, which door the skeleton-key is for!

(Translated by Andaleeb)

TUNNEL

I haven't seen tunnels, but you. I've got some
firestones, stuffed birds, bubble-making devices
and so on. Are you regaining your trust now?
Trains full of soldiers are headed to the frontier.
Let's close our eyes and see all these. How would
you see a new world if you don't see the stature
of your good old banyan-tree. At night, I hear
zillions of filthy flies' buzz around us. You haven't
explained yet why you used to carry a razor-sharp
hacksaw blade in bed consistently.

(Translated by Andaleeb)

PREFACE

"A poem is never finished, only abandoned." – Paul Valery

May this afternoon's feeble shadows fall upon all the heady lines of my poetry, or may heaps of dry leaves blaze up in flames beside them today. On return, the hunter will see nothing but ashes flying to and from.

How much of truth ever comes up near pleasure? I tell those driven out of a pilgrimage that all I've wished is to stuff the broken violin with all my sins.

May those birds, too, come back now, those that flew from the groves of mouri-flowers towards the sea.

On a terribly quiet night, you've known, especially after every kiss, that the weight of this foggy existence becomes a little lighter. Crested cocks and lyres – these were our last assets. Why do you hide away when the maddening rush of zebras starts! Should you wait a little, you'll see how a lonely drop of dew dissolves into the earth slowly, falling down the trunk of any of the tall trees lined along the edge of a path strewn with dead leaves and dead flowers on a morning.

See more, a few unknown birds often come up to roost
among our olive trees, the birds I mistake for
philosophers of a millennium before or after.

(Translated by Sofiul Azam)

MY SCHOOL

What is a watch's influence in infinite time, thinking that i have a bit of headache around teatime? To relief, then i sit on a marigold decor boat. Her sailor, often smiling propose me to enter underworld. I do not agree at all, because if there the world is infinite too, then? Rather let's visit that ever-floating sea-whores home. Time, underworld and body's she is the ultimate teacher.

(Translated by Tanvir Ratul)

A BOOK HAS A BANG

A book has a bang and a final bathe in the blue tinge.

I settled in puzzling fear to go both

in the edge of summer night.

And the fear that draws me

lies deep in Snake-Ladder game and

I see a desert- philosopher turns to scarecrow by night.

As if immense beckoning of book seems

as the peacock's call.

As if horrified by earth-- as if a hidden liquor.

 I find jewels in his eyes through millions of skies.

The moon comes to

count every particle of my body and

I go to non-space where shades red.

A fake lion, a fake island suddenly

throws me in the prison of thoughts

We-- me and the white door-guard bird wait idle

Craggy paths of letters

of the stunned peahen and night kneading peacock.

(Translated by Mosabbir Ahe Ali)

THE ISLAND OF DELIGHT

Sometimes I remember the island of delight.
Everywhere move hundreds of ducks losing their
vulgarity. There form the beds of falling mauve leaps.
Like the continuous aerial weeping of fox,
you are no longer a ordinary nomadic.
The birds who are the jack
of all trades return and argue.
In the next morning,
there rises the singing head of Orpheus.
Then why are you making Harp?
Why are you putting dizzy buttons and
white pebbles in secret basket?
The grapes and Sonnets
are the waste of ripening still in somewhere!

A blind scarecrow sings
an insatiable song in variety of tunes. Today you

seem the King of Sands, gradually becoming a
homeless, aimless and deposed of breast.
Who knows about whom depth? Now in

his bow of eyebrow, there he hides the concealed truth.

Then comes the final stanza.

Being cleaned away blood drops from

Holy Grayle, there only remains the

seed, shell and fills with bitter sweet lines.

Take your marble box with you; wait

in slope under the flower tree,

Writing you as gold, there begins the hunting at night.

[Translated by Mosabbir Ahe Ali]

SHAH ALAM DULAL

Date of Birth: 02 September

Place of Birth: Vikrampur, Bangladesh

Education: Master of Management

Publication: 02

Lives: in New York, USA.

Email: shahalamdulal777@gmail.com

FREEDOM

Searching dictionaries for the freedom's meaning
My blood rushes to my ears, my eyes widening!
Freedom's supposed to be living on rice and fish
Freedom supposed to be able to pen my wish.
Freedom supposes the people own the nation.
Allowing my mind to free diction.
Freedom means the right to life
Changing our rulers shall be our fief.
Freedom means development's smile
No hangings ordered at the drop of a file.
Freedom means the benign touch of peace and joy
The 'Padma' and 'Korotoa' shall flow in lazy ploy.
Freedom means no disparity
Freedom only means, we all are Bangladeshi.

Now I see

Freedom's gone from the dictionary
Freedom stands for inhuman cruelty
Freedom stands for a ban on speech
Freedom stands for treading a narrow path

Freedom is listening only to the queen's wrath
There are no freedoms beyond these.

[Translated by: Iftikhar Ahmed Nasir]

FROM GARDEN TO POT

A thousand cuttings sweat and tears

Made a huge garden room;

To make a single rose bloom.

Somehow, somewhere something went wrong

Laid the garden low, nor 'wester strong.

Blooms adorn that garden not

The flower moving to an earthen pot.

Don't know how

The flower's doing now.

[Translated by: Iftikhar Ahmed Nasir]

GOODBYE

Hello there, well that is, Hi.
Before knowing, how could
You just say goodbye?
Against the whipping wind,
Flying is not easy.
Though I'm near to you,
You claim to be busy.
As for me, I'm holding
In the deepest sigh,
And as for you, now
I'm saying goodbye.

[Translated by: Ruma Alam]

LETTER TO NANDINI

Nandini, I'm not near
And wonder how you are?
With the afternoon sun's rays
Beating down on you.
Are you aimlessly shifting
Sands and pebbles from the rice?
Start the dinner, tiredness Cripple
In Cradle in the rattan
Swing on veranda hidden quietly
By the window listening to the footsteps?
Respite from all the pressure, I write.
I write to you with a heavy heart
Holding the cup of tea, you made me.
The taste lingers forever, sip by sip.
Expectation is like holding your breath waiting.
Gather my courage and make my attempt
To get to know you.
Nervous anticipation bated breath
You captured my heart with your response
Like a deer caught in the headlight.
Your world has entranced me

I am enchanted and entangled.

I wonder about trivial things, practical things.

Did you turn off the lights?

Do you take pleasure in your music?

Do you talk about me with your acquaintances?

Do you count the days since we were together?

My heart beats with the rhythm of pain.

I must end now.

My love flies to you like a flock of birds.

[Translated by: Ruma Alam & Maherukh]

SOUND OF TEARS

I'm well and living too

Though, perhaps, not as well as you.

My eyes are open

No need for blindfold games

To (truly) know men.

What's the use of saying

I am unwell, unblest

When it matters not to anyone in the least.

He who knows, understands

You cannot convey what the mind wants.

Knowing I'm well and good

You'll be better off in your solitude.

Tell me then mistress,

Why will I be in grief to cause you distress?

[Translated by: Iftikhar Ahmed Nasir]

STRAIGHT EQUATION

Your visions blurred
You see me not.
Ceaselessly saying Gold
Of the glittered copper.
Simple steps are hard for you
Complications you forte,
Who will be to blame
If accidents come?
Delve into your mind
To find what you really want.
Before you leave,
Know where you want to go.

[Translated by: Iftikhar Ahmed Nasir]

THE DISTANCE

Missed out this summer too,
On Jones or Orchard beach,
Though we're both here
Under the same sky, you and me.
Savory plates of City Island,
Mashed potato and Salmon
Gave our table set a pass.
As I did leis of Bokul to don.
If we, ever we meet
At some soiree or a poet's fairs
Perhaps, you will secretly sob
At the distance that separated
You and me.

[Translated by: Ruma Alam]

THE GAMES

Win or lose
A must in any civilized game.
You and I could've been engrossed
In domestic Snakes & Ladders,
Or lost in pocketing plastic carom men.

Do you know chess?
If you don't, let it be; there
are enough card games for two.
Wouldn't've been difficult to play for high stakes
And hand over your winnings at my loss.
No regret to bring me to tears.

Hide and Seek, Cops and Robbers,
so many childhood games
We two could've joyously played
To startle some hard-found moments of freedom.

We could have singing, rhyming and staring contests
Matching our wits too. Invitations to make believe
Cookouts In the afternoon.

With so many games to choose from,
Why did you play with the keepsake heart?

[Translated by: Iftikhar Ahmed Nasir]

TREASURED WISH

I'll descend into twenty-eight
You stay on twenty-three
Then will my days begin (to)
To & from you will see.
Like boiling blood, spurting out
It'll declare its love to earth.
I'll be the heedless youth,
If you are before me
You lean on your window
And call out softly.
On stealthy feet
Your hand I'll tie
In bed, for a thousand years
We will lie.

[Translated by: Iftikhar Ahmed Nasir]

WORD HAD IT

Word had it- I'd bequeathed all of my share to you.

They're nobodies, Rani, Mita or Shumi.

Word had it- Green flowers

would grace green gardens

Our only abode on land and water.

Word had it- No matter the tempests of havoc

Colored dreams would canoe on blue oceans.

Word had it- We'd scale the far hills of solitude

Gorge on lotus in the pouring rain.

Word had it- You'd climb trees to pick orchids

Finding the strength in the bosom of love.

Word had it- Where faeries and reeds teem

We'll honeymoon on a raft

of the moon.

Word had it

Beside the discovered world

A new abode we'll build in days to com.

[Translated by: Iftikhar Ahmed Nasir]

AHMED JAMIL

Date of Birth:

Place of Birth: Dhaka Bangladesh

Education:

Publication: 01

Live in: New York, USA

Email:

THE LINE OF LIFE

Always there is tug of war with temporary life

I want to go the forest

Leaving worldly bond for rest

Love and affection not real

They follow destructive serial

The affection of mother

Gives the children a moment's pleasure

The conversation with wife

Is dramatic: But not last long in the life

Still we are to obey the order

The order of our creature.

We are to do our duty

To add glory and beauty

We are to follow the social norms

We are to abide by the love and other forms

If not, we will not go to paradise

We must avoid here on earth crime and vice.

FLOWER

I dream of flower

As I loved them so clearly

I love them with all my heart sincerely

Flower are to me very near

They are dearest than dear

I forgot of my lover

In the scent of flower

I want to give flower perpetual longevity

But I failed miserably in my activity

One day the flower lost their freshness

They were dried up and died in harness

I could not keep them in my breast

For them it most secured nest

Creating a pathetic scene

They were thrown in the dustbin

Time kills everything

Nothing remains for human being.

AFTER MY DEATH

After my death don't decorate my funeral pyre

Don't give rose water or scented on my grave

Don't bury me in a costly grave yard

nothing should be for dead man

the body will be rotten and reduce to dust

of what use the of body would come?

Don't spend money for me

Give my belongings in the charity

Bury me bare body as I came

here on earth through the belly grave

of my mother

If so my soul will get peace.

WHERE IS HEAVEN

I am anxious to know about heaven

As I am suffocated in a polluted atmosphere

Muggers raise their pistols around me

Bandits pulled out the ear rings from my beloved wife

Unclean talks are going on in the movie theatre

I don't want the fairies of the heaven

I want shady spot of the heaven

Where i can rest peaceful

My face been burnt by the heat of this society

I would like to get rid of it.

I WILL FIND OUT

Year after year I am walking and walking
Row of bomb burning trees looking and looking
The hungry beggar collecting food from dustbin
For food men are fighting and committing sin
I have seen the war-torn battle field
Where men women children were killed
House were burning in flames
Men were indulging in destructive games
Mother was calling her dead child
The environment was polluted and wild
I was nothing but a helpless observer
A baby was sucking the breast of his dying mother
I am in search of a peace city
Where there's peace no atrocity
Where there's no violence or ugliness
I am searching for that city with all eagerness.

A GUEST FOR A MOMENT

I am walking continuously
I don't know my destination
The path just beyond me
does not come to in front
it remains in the back
I gaze back hundred times
I can't go back to farmer life
Where is the last destination of the human being?
Where is the barricade?
Men are travelling and travelling
Travelling is a continuous process
Men are going never to come
Human moment is endless
He will be walking up to last day of life.

THE CLERK

My heart is always heavy with want and miseries
I am small clerk fighting against poverty
My wife and my children are depended on me
I cannot fulfill their wish
I can't feed them well
I can't give theme proper education
I can't clothe them
They are clad in tatters
Prices of commodities in the market are very high
They are out of my reach
My family members eagerly wait
to see what I bought for them
from the market
Good marketing makes them happy
Bad marketing makes theme sad
I never think that I shall be a well to do man
I only pray to god
Allow me and the members
of my family to live in the midst
of want and sufferings.

PRISONER OF WORK

You are imprisoned in the working area
About bird's freedom you have no idea
You have not seen the beauty of blooming flowers
In the midst of dense fogs, the lofty towers
You have not seen sweet moonlit night
Natural beauty gone out of your sight
All through life you were submerged in working pool
Work has made you complete fool
Have you walked down
holding the hand of your lover
In the open lane in your youthful age ever?
Have you played with your mates in boyhood?
Have you got the love of your wife in happy mood?
You spend your life running after money
You had no time to taste the love of honey
You have killed the beautiful side of your life
For the sake money you lost your wife
You have not seen the beauty of nature
You have not enjoyed human atmosphere
You never tried to see the other side of the river
You have deprived yourself in hard labour.

ALAM SIDDIQUE

Date of Birth: 28 May 1981

Place of Birth: Gaibandha, Bangladesh

Education: Master of Social Science

Publication: 08

Live in: New York, USA

Email: Siddique528@gmail.Com

MONALISA

My Lady or Monalisa's sobs or smile
The Answer Is Here, I hear with full horror
Researcher's research then stops instantly
All the thinking unknowingly, make me puzzled.

The question arises, how Vinci paint image of his lady
The biggest painting took sixteen years to complete
Nobody knows whom he portrayed in the painting
There are lots of mystery surrounds
with Mona Lisa painting.

Alien's face is behind the Mona Lisa's face
The smile of child's, its happiness or pleasure
It 's protected with bullet proof glass frame
Monlisa is covered with spotless Security.

ALIVE STONE

Beside the seashores of the Europe and America
Sailing Stone can walk past alone
They also have the name of Running Rock
To see them you've to go near the sea.
Moving Stone does not go i straight line
Don't think it's moving in a chariot.
It will move diagonally either right or left
Leaving a long track, it moves downwards.
The people of the area say it is sign of good luck
They keep the beach guarded and follows the signal
Even thirty hundred kilograms stones also move
The question is, how these stones move so easily
The running rock tells about the movement of storm
To look at this matter people gather in the sea shore
Stone is static, but how the run do you know?
This is happening due
to the weather condition, you know.

BROTHER ISLAND

The laughter of ghosts can be heard
in an island named Brother
Like human beings they are coughing
If you go to the island, you'll shiver in your heart
Why this ghost kingdom started, you know?

Brother Island was
having dwelling houses of the people
Once a great epidemic broke out there
People ran away in fear of ghosts
People were drowned due to a huge tidal boar

From distance iit is like a Dream land
If you go near it's a Death Valley
If the person enters in the cave their mouths get locked
If one goes to the island, no one is happy

The dead man's crying sound is heard in the day
White clothed people walk around laughing
The fire burns blazing at midnight
Since then people call it a ghost kingdom.

RAINBOW RIVER

The river that came down from heaven is called Kano
Rainbow colors are poured
down on the river, you know?
Many colors are playful in the river water
All colors mingle with water and game of color is seen.

If you go to Colombia you can see the river by yourself
Your eyes will fill with joy, and you heart with awe
It seems, you were sitting in the middle water
And a full sail boat is floating with rippling sound

River water comes down from the mountain
As if dancing like a young petit girl
Water moves on in rippling sound as if a flute is sing
Your wayward heart will be softened with peace.

KUBAIR PADDY

The town Kubair Paddy is built under the ground
In Australia, the city is filled with mysteries
Snakes and lizards wee abound before the people live,
In the nineteen eleven people have come to say here

Under the desert, there is a mine full of gems
Tiger's eyes dazzle on the opal stones
There were n trees, no oil at all
There are opal stones abounds all around.
Opal floats in bundles in the water
The miner-worker rushed to take those out
They must move a long way to reach there
It's not as easy as the crow fly?
Thus, the workers build
up their dwellings under the ground
In severe winter it's not easy to come here and go back.
The city grew like a cave under the ground
Now it has developed to attract peoples interest.

MERMAID

One half is like a fish the other is a woman
They live in water, their home is in the water
We all know them as mermaids
They look at us in enchanting gaze as if smiling
They bask in sea beach and lives in te water
They love water like the fishes.
Some were caught in the nets of the fisher-men
Their smiling is beautiful, they have cute dimples too
They live very silently all by themselves
Sometimes they also fall in love, loves the family,
Living in boundless ocean, they entwine in love
They draw a perfect picture of love?

No one knows whether it's rumors or true
The scientists did not get any proof they avoid it
The mermaids are there, something is there,
The scents are still looking in the depth of ocean
The eyes of everyone look for it in the sea
It's mystery? or mermaid? No one knows.

QUEEN MARIE

There was a phantom ship called Queen Mary
It did not delay in crossing the ocean
It crossed the Atlantic in merely five days
All the passengers of were happy to buy Mary's tickets.
From the beginning, people could
see white shadow of ghosts
Phantom or a body is sitting on deck
At times, suddenly, flute s played by ghost
Sometimes loud weird laughter can be heard

This ship was made for World War
Many things of the Queen Mary were Hostile
Worldwide weird news spread of Queen Mary,
Then the American soldiers used this ship
Queen Mary got rammed killing three soldiers
Do the dead soldiers create problem in the ship
These ideas all spread among boarders of the ship
 They saw the shadows
of ghosts in the day, night and morn.

DERINQUU

There was a city in Turkey below the ground level
People of that city fled away somewhere else
The eighteen story of the city were below the ground
The city of Derinquzu is not unknown at all.

Darikuzu was covered by sol all around
It looked like a military base
The door is closed by a stone
Who made such a city in ancient time?

The secret city of Derinkuzu was made in ancient times
There is no problem though the weather is hostile
This city is named as dhupchaya in fairy tales time
People are going to see the city groups.

SELF-MURDER FOREST

There was a Suicide Forest in the country called Japan
When somebody is depressed he goes there to die
If someone goes to that forest once,
he does not return again
Who have the courage to go to that man-eater forest?

Anybody kills himself in that Suicide forest
Will anyone get such a quiet
environment in the house?
Suicide Forest is also called Sea of Plant
Between the tree the dead souls move around.

Some people claim this forest as Satan Forest as well
When some takes a car there he loses the car's keys
Darkness covers the area gradually in the day time
It's difficult to come back from this forest
to this difficult life from the forest.
After reading the novel Kuroye Kai Ju
The readers intend to suicide
Number of suicides are rising every year
The Japanese loses to themselves in silence.

DOLL ISLAND

Three children were playing with the dolls one day
A supernatural power took away one of them
The child was found in a secluded pond on the place
Then people gradually discarded the island totally

For a long time, the place remained devoid of people
The owls reside on the trees, crows only call out
In the day time the place seems gloomy and dark,
 A child's wailing sound
can be heard, calling her mother

Priest July went there to to contemplate in section
In the island of Mexico, she had nightmare and freight
Suddenly, Julian felt shivering, he hearts ached
A spirit started crying loudly at mid night.

The soul of dead child comes and wants tattered doll
She whimpered and at times laughed out loudly
She demanded to Julian a doll without a leg
July priest returns to main land in that pursuit.

She goes to every house and asked to give her a doll
Only the dolls without hand or leg, is what she asked
She vended vegetable and bought more dolls
She decorated the entire island with those dolls.

[Translated by Siddique Mahmudur Rahman]

SHAKIL REAZ

Date of Birth: 17 October 1970

Place of Birth: Dhaka, Bangladesh

Education: Master of Mass Communication and Journalism

Publication: 07

Lives in: Stockholm, Sweden

Email: shakil.reaz@gmail.com

WINTER MELODY

White-robed winter comes in and stayed
The seasons of earth stopped in this country
The snow-topped houses are
Like white cap of the Huzurs
And there are melodies of Milad! Kulkhani!
This city died of heart disease
Snow lies on the steps like shroud of the dead
As if is sitting silently for being cremated
Beside the coffin, we're moving like incense-sticks
Our breaths are like incense-fragrance
Move through the air.

You drew a heart on the bonnet of the car
And wrote your lover's name
New snow covered that too
In your country the world is so colorful
Country of you colorful-damsels the season change
You experience Kartik, Fagun brings savor

Your seasons are flowing endlessly, as you're
Here earth is old lady, posture is brooding

Here winter has Alzheimer

Here winter has come to forget its destination

In this city, O Earth, your season has stopped, Alas!

SEASON

Under these red, blue, green attachments
Weird sobbing night returns again and again
In that night we illuminated sparse moment
A bowl full of milk, Firefight in the front like a wick
We left behind a few puffs
That night returns in full moon. In that light
I, like a poor bacterium turn your milk into whey
Like this my organic life is consumed by murderers
I breath my last on my death, i come
Wiping out the definition of living
I made my embryo made by heart
Embryo didn't assimilate that
So, I made it return to my blood
I wiped my mouth; I put into my mouth a bite
Green bank of savings I keep some residue
Damsels, that means this moonbeam are wretched
That means night waned under the candle-light
That means we divided your secret seasons
Under the celebration of season-less night.

TWO CLUTCHES

Before the death the life meandered

How could you make it turn away

It happens in Autumn,

The leaves shed down at dead of night

Orange leaves, lying, a pale moonlight

Leaves some soft melodies

I take the tune on my guitar

Your ayes are struck on the guitar, you're dying

You follow widely

Your unruly eyes turned like screw and

Turned loose.

Death become sharper in this blindness

Before the death the life meandered

In the posture of prayer

I closed my ten fingers of both the palms

Hoping, you'll loan me two of your clutches

Two clutches! Shall you offer me this hunger?

I'm famished, lying in a plate, a few bits of food

How could you resist?

MY NEW YEAR

I stare at the movement of hours, days and year

Milky Way yawns and drives away their own ghosts

It broods like the top

The universe inflates more

It occupies some more unknown quarters

This swelling in weighed accurately

So, the new year comes and goes precisely

My time remain as my own

My year stayed static waiting in queue.

POSTURE THAT CALLED LOVE

I wipe out my life with the eraser of suicide
I think life is a sin, the breaths those are
Inscribes in my palms
Life that are written in my fate,
I want to spill something
Who will pick that up?

A black crane comes and salutes me.
If my palms turn into my bed, in that bed
Beside the marriage-line silently lies
A faint line lies
Who is calling me? t says, how long you rested?
How much is pretension?
How much life remained in life?
Still its life! In this line lurches the fate
Then? Why then the Mystic says,
After all, happiness is there in the end,
Marriage is imminent.

One body is trembling softly under another body
This posture is called love.

I've left this posture in my early days
under the tree, in Gorachand Road;
Today at Eskaton, Dilu Road, they came back
As an elder.

FOR WHOM, I KNOW NOT

Every time I weep for you, the more I think of you
In each weeping, each time my loving thoughts
One by one star glazes up in faraway sky
Then the night would be illuminated
More than a day.
There'll be no night left!
There'll be only one day, the bright noon only
I don't wish such weird thought in my heart, never
One day if t really happens come haunting, I fear
I do not think infinite
Worrying, I made some stars feel asleep
I want to play with you in two palms of dark nights.

CROSS EYED

I just poured my mischievous Inattention on your hasty attitude. Your breakup has blown up your strange beautiful cross-eyes. Last month we talked about cross-eyes. Penelope Cruz, Salma Hayek etc. You said yes, they're lucky. Then one of your eyes was looking into my one eye and the other eye aimed at my ear. And was very shining. Today I avoided your eyes entire day.

At the end of the day, while I was tiding up the table, I asked, do you want to tell me, Cat

She pouted her lips and said, No. Leave it, nothing serious. I don't need anything.

I felt, you wanted to say, you've

a lot to say. You need a lot.

LETTER

Pen name was more beloved than our own name

I sent a letter to the storm that

language was never a verse

Starting writing letter to me, I was sick

In the middle, it was dark, I turn into envelope.

Nude women were following you in the envelope

Those who called, are valiant

Aren't they proud of the parade?

It is humiliation; the main thing is self-conscious sex

On the deepest path, the silence of pensive astronauts

But is i the posture of weaving,

fashion, and everything is obscene?

In pretense of love, copper iron, stone age spell?

Who knows the depth of soil,

how much is wet or fertile

How much pyramid, how's mummy,

how far deep to go for disease?

How much is the floor, its wounds,

alone I water the land

The left bosom is exhausted, famished,

the pain of complications

I remember you soaked in sari on rain

I forget you in the sunshine, the rays save annihilation.

The letter is very intimidating, so your name is implied

The pseudonym was not found,

I left the attempt of search

I have written so much but know

the wailing of loneliness

The poetry could not have been

the art of the rules itself.

LOOK HERE, PARU

On the palm, I light the willful lamp
Look here Paru
How precarious we are here Devdas
Needless unfortunate in
the name of some young people
We cannot give our lovable youth to anyone and
In the night of Paus under one diseased trees
Standing alone awakes downfall. This is life,
All the others are deaths, this keeping awake is
an unprecedented breath, in a polite death.
In our face, bosom, eyes, hair, eyes, beards, tears
Condensed clouds do not come down as rains anytime
The long corridor of moss-covered Zamindar house
All the guard are burnt with long end of sari
Somebody came with the sound of tingling of bangles
Do not bow down after our last breath,
Senseless body fall crying is head scuffle on the head
So, the corpse wail, cry scorched mystery,
and excited fever
Who has come to avoid this fever? Chandramukhi?
And under the morbid moon light our dried blood

Are measured with which thermometer?
And our oozing fever, these uncertain ones
Leaving our failures if we escape, then is it called death
Look her, Paru.

THE HOUSE NEXT DOOR

I look through the window
I see even in this midnight you are heaving in gasping
Fumbling in the dark today I told a painful fairy tale
To the Maple tree of your yard
Maple weep, Maple heave long sighs
Like this I ooze out oxygen from the Maple for you
O you girl with breathing problem,
Are you getting oxygen properly, now?
Look! If not, tomorrow night I will tell Maple
The heartbreaking story of our alphabets.

[Translated by Siddique Mahmudur Rahman]

QUAZI ABRAR JOHIR

Date of Birth: 28 April 1997

Place of Birth: Dhaka, Bangladesh

Education: BSc. Engineering [3rd Grade]

Living in: New York, USA

Email: Quazi.johir@gmail.com

SHY FLOWER

Oh, won't you open
Spread your petals
And welcome them?

Oh, won't you open,
And shower us
With your radiance?

Oh, won't you open,
And entice us
With your scent?

Oh, won't you open,
And delight us
In your presence?

A MOMENT

Tick tock
The clock
Ticks
My mind fills to the brim,
Until my thoughts spill
Out

I am stripped,
Of all flesh and bone
Till I am left with nothing
But a phone
To my self

In the distance a stream flows
Just as the blood
In my fleshless body
And for a moment a flood,
Next my woes
Come flooding back to me.

Butterflies in my stomach

No sensations in my feet
Birds chirping in the distance,
My posture slightly beats

I wake up from my trance.

NEW LEAF

Let us venture then
Into ephemerality,
Of desperate skies
And dimly lit streets
Hubbubs of crowds
Endless coffee meets.

Laughter one moment, tears the next,
The story of time, ingrained in text.

Through the evening, and into the night,
The celebration commenced, not a soul in sight.

And then they arrived, in their masses and huddles,
I stared, I envied and I cried a puddle.

And I wondered, was it my hair?
Or was it my torn blazer
How it hung off the chair?
The night went on
A void of joy,

Empty promises
And pale faces
Half empty glasses
Next to golden chalices.

THE CREATURE

Don't fear them
Little red robin wren
Soar all freely to Bethlehem
Birthplace of great men
Seek shelter in you hardened shell
From the creature that in the corner, dwells

Now see how he ensnares,
As though he does not care
See through your innocence
He shall do so kindly.
Leave you senseless
And torture you blithely.

Now in your destruction
His power shall arise,
Deny him the satisfaction
And lead him to demise.

CHILDREN OF THE FIRE

Alas! I cannot hold it in any longer
Nature forbade
Curiosity encouraged
Slim edged blade,
An offspring was born and was bred
Within the flames of extinction.

Still they pondered
With what perplexity to approach
These kindred,
Untamed roach?

For it to blossom,
Ozymandias, king of kings
Or David
Victim of misconception?

To what depths this fire will burn,
Shall only be determined,
By the web with which
It was spurn.

DIVINITY

She was a Goddess
And I, a prophet
Love was a crisp note
Slid into my pocket

To be delivered
Prompt and unopened
But the love of sin
Led me astray

And in this note
I saw demise
With anger He wrote
But His heart still cries

So I ran and ran
Till the end of Time
My Goddess teary
Her eyes like lime

In this unknown land

They took me stray
2 meals daily
My handsome pay

Forgiveness I sought
Reconnect with divine
One sharp sweep
It gushed like wine

The end, the end.
Last ounce of pain
Fate repeated itself
It began again.

FAKIR SELIM

Date of Birth: 14 April

Place of Birth: Narail, Bangladesh

Education: Master of Public Administration

Living in: Washington DC

Email: fakirselimusa@gmail.com

E DEVICE

One little device
Ruling bullying fooling us and
pulling our price;

Flowing through the air
Glowing front and rear
Slowing our speed as if
human are its gear;

Shaking us as toys
Adults girls and boys
Baking like bacon spike
faking with joys;

Silly little device
Controlling us as ice
Sometimes as friendly while
sometime in disguise;

Wherever you are
home rome or car

Device will detect you
even though too far;

Are you in a lunch?
On the floor of dance?
You might be caught by someone
Without any chance;

Even when sick
People give a click
E device is very nice
above all the pick;

Starting from the birth
On this very earth
Everything is controlled
From franklin to Perth.

DON'T CALL OLD

Don't call me old;
I have seen all the treasures
diamonds and gold;

I spent countless cent
Millions of money
Experience the ages change
from bitter to honey;

Calling me old now?
Not knowing the know-how?
The universe is moving fast
And you are old tomorrow.

LOL

Like comment love or hate
Lovely words of virtual net
Facebook has made them all hot
No use of comma, space dot.

power shower sour even sweet
All have been keen to become tweet
Joke folk and emotions of soul
Facebook has made them all lol.

Breaking news talk show views
Almost all out of use
Social media Wikipedia ruling our age
Generation is locked up in unseeable cage.

SAD

I am sad Being a dad
Hungry for a letter,
From my son But no one
Whatever is the matter,
But alas not a buzz
Writing me through air,
Now a day People say
This is not fair;

Ink of the pen
Abandoned in vein
Left behind for none,
Getting his notes
Highlighted quotes
By emails and notes of fun;

Chatting on the phone
From isolated zone
But one can see the other,
'Oh dear son
Peace be upon'

Blessings to son by Mother;

'My Dear dad
Do not be sad'
Words of letters are gone,
Instead of those
poems and prose
The words are short and shun;

The daughters and sons
The Jennifers and Johns
Are addict and tricked by web,
They do not know how
The civilization now
confined in computer lab;

Contact of masses
Among all the classes
Are increasing without doubt,
daughter and son
Caring for none
Are keeping the families out.

PRESS FREEDOM

Freedom of press
Has a lot of stress?
Terms and conditions applied
With biased laws supplied;

With Influence of rulers on press
Publishing of papers by their grace
No one knows what are the gains?
Why do they always sell their brains?

Mass people pass their time
Reading the mass media's,
stories of crime;

Mostly with no wonder,
rarely breaking news
Drawing the attention of readers in huge;

And the rest, is all the best,
Pressure from the elites and rulers,
Expressed in talk shows with

Lots of colors;

On the live show, whatever you know,
You are not allowed to tell anything raw;

If off the track, biting their back,
there's no mercy dear,
you will be sacked;
If media is rusted
and nowhere' s trusted
The virtual world dances
with innovative chances;

The Facebook and viber and Twitter,
These are the big parties and our fighter,
They created the viewers
and readers and writers;

When mass media rides
on donkeys and Cars,
The Millennials' miles are counted on Mars;
Even the patients in coma,
Coming out dancing,

forgetting their trauma;

And still our mass media then,

Looking for news in the bedrooms and den.

SHUKLA GANGULI

Date of Birth: 21 November

Place of Birth: Kolkata, India

Education: Bachelor Degree

Publication:

Living in: Maryland, USA

Email: Shuklaganguli@gmail.com

WORDS

I spoke that word only for word sake
Maiden moon and innumerable
stars were still above us
Verses were dispersed into
fiction or fiction into my verses.

An unsigned covert alliance was in there
Illustrated or immaculately crafted sentences,
Speechless cartographic!
The dust-splattered curtain of the window
And its outside, clouds are floating away
Through the unbounded horizon -
Like a few anonymous stanzas.

GAMES OF SHADES IN DARKNESS

In the unfathomable blind ally
I would like to come back
Once again

Raiding on lighted waves of Moonlight
Scented with fragrance of blue-flowers
Once again
I would like to come back
Awaken late in the night
To wavering shadows of light and darkness

The norm of measuring the
understanding or misunderstanding,
The scale of partiality and fluctuations
The forge of the blacksmith, smithery of red-hot iron
Burning desires of hammering
Sizzling fire of turmoils of life
And the serpent movement of the faraway train
In overlong vacation to prepare self in my own way
With very failure of wellbeing
Staying alive with arguments,

protests, pity and charity!

I'm unable to explain anyone that

Me, no longer

Do not love myself anymore

MELANCHOLY

Melancholy-, why you do embrace me
While I'm roaming around
the boundary lines of the field
Barefooted I'm and dressed on barely nothing

Over there, by the Shirish-Tree, corner to the field;
Where there, into every drop of rain
I could see you, my Melancholy

As in a lonely balcony
Flocks of pigeons lined in rows, rest in silence

The glowing spectrums overflow during late dusk

Only Ether into air
In a sudden blow of wind- inhale with full of life
Then let the golden butterfly fly away

LOST MELODIES

Lost melodies-; fear of losing is
All over the figure with made of wax

In exuberance, childish play of the doom
Plays sounds of rain all through-,
In the pages of red-blue-gold
With the foil-plated canvas of life are
Turbulence of the foamy ocean-waves;
Gradually fading-away
into white of decaying domestic life
Turmoiling over profound moonlighted forest!

Lost fears-, lost melodies of
Raga Emon-Voyrob
Tuning over cell-to-cell of the body

Through eternity...
The nocturnal birds are
Supposed not to be sing, not at all.

MY DREARY

The wake-up dreary, my drowsy eyes looking for you
Bonfire burning the forest in Sayadri Mountain Range
Making waves of sparkling fire in the dark

Nocturnal birds flap their wings
Momentarily they become
A collage of thousand faces of flood-victims
A sunken ship floats up again
My dreary, come along, let me hug you!

LAXMAN-REKHA

Restrictions were there - to cross
the mythical drawn line
I didn't listen; Me, wanted
to experience it by touching -
Only what I saw from behind the closed-blinds-, was
Frustration stricken skeletal humans are
Seems bargaining for life

Musical sounds of the nonstop rain
Evokes the affection for smoking cigarette;
Was there any hints of fire in to sparkling?

THE GAME OF LOVE

Like to roam from the deep to into the deepest
As it is a warship, nurtured by the sailor
Count-downing to come back to the shore,
The danger signals, flashes of blood in cold breeze,
Mirage images of sky at the telescope-sight
And abundance of Ultramarine into water below
The cheers for victories of successfully
Overcome obstructions,
Rotted love life
Trying to review the naked truths of life by
Dipping in Kerosene, over and over mistakes are
Still trying to advance forward
with paying for mistakes
Unconditional love-; not longing for anything
Who is the biggest multiplying factor
Being afraid of solving numbers-
Does it ever been calculated correctly?
In the ongoing periods of time-,
Playing 'Games of Love' is nothing but
Fall of rhythm, is an unaccomplished World
Full of unsparing emptiness.

WHO IS OVER THERE

The final rays from the Sun, setting to west
Playing a hide and seek
Over the boundless horizon
Who knows where the destinations are,
Was there were any destination at all?

Leading a life like a horse-shoe
In lie-in-to dust break yard
Or the starry garlands of Goddess
Or to the playground of sparkling-crackling fireworks
Or being suppressed mechanical life
Was there were any life at all-

The cliché expressions of newspapers
From the dark moon of lunar phases
Quietly flowing to waning eleventh-crescent
Passing across the eternity ...
Was there were the Eternity at all-
Closing my eyes, try to enjoy
Amazing postures of the classical dancer
Full of dalliance

The lonely sign of age on tune-rhythm-tempo

Through the fallen fringe, can see the contexture waist

Waving naked anticipation of motherhood

Which destination must go

Who knows

Was there were any destination at all

The mythical Jewel on the serpent's crown

Playing hide and seek

Into the boundless horizon ...

Who is over there-?

FERTILITY OF THE DESERT

Even after sharp thrones are pulled-out
Blood-stained root was still there,
With affections for loosen soil-, Belly-button
 Sucking the neiva smell of the wet-soil

Dancing and whistling,
The long-tailed Drongo and Nightingale
Pick-up those rays of Sunshine
That were vibrating on the leaves
As to promise for staying alive

Me-, I'm that very fertility of the desert.

POISON

Perfect replica of the moss-grown Hemlock cup

The overcasting Smokey Autumn evening

Of Kolkata

With

The games of right and wrong.

You told, God might know-, looking for Him days over

With perpetual anticipations

When the rain washes down

Deep green leaves of Trot flower

Clouds are coming down

To Lonavla local train

After waiting all through the night

Have gotten the blanket of stars

Once a while

I probably found my God-;

3:55 local train

Vast red of Regia flowers and

No hurry at all

You belongs-, to my entity

Like Socrates!

SHEULI JAHAN

Date of Birth: 10 August 1970

Place of Birth: Dhaka, Bangladesh

Education: Master of Political Science

Publication: 02

Lives in: Toronto, Canada

Email: jahansheuli@gmail.com

HENCE LIFE LONG IMPRISONMENT

Everyday has a tomorrow
Every yesterday has a today
After tomorrow, no days remain there,
That day neither you, nor me,
There remain endless hollow.

Look, once every day, I leave the residence of poetry
I fall off from stem, associated with the stars
The stars don't return; but I am
bound to turn again and again.
I start to compose the numerals from the beginning,
Searching the words from old to modern.
I submerge into quicksand
of poems; and float for the future.
Handful of air-balloon crumble in the fist.
The dense breath of anticipation agitates the artery.
Oh, firefly! do not sacrifice
in the fire of desired Diwali;
Let some colorful neon light burn-
That tiny light might enlighten the darkness,
 Showing the ways of success, of creation

Let a few futures are erected

I spread my cloth and got the wings of sea-gull

How I can leave lifelong thirst or debt?

Hence, accept my life long imprisonment.

IMPOVERISHED

The bird fly wiping their beaks on the sand

They leave their feathers, and become exhausted.

The feather does not look for the bird

And the birds do not search for its feathers.

In the homeless river water

the wonders of the moon remain awake

Shadows walk past through the Mahua and honey

The shadows leave behind the whistle of conk

The traveler might return in the corners of setting sun,

The path – does it really returns?

The flowers keep the vow

Those who fly away they make everything destitute.

HISTORY OF MELANCHOLIC EFFIGY

Human being passes away-
Leaving behind merely the past in the empty room,
A few incompleteness and a few expecting sighs.
Some breath and edifice swing continuously
with the pendulum
In the distance of the breath
Our lives, colorful Arabic scripts
cover all through the life
Quavering by the green dewdrops and
flickering the complex theories of life
Thrown away to eternity in a momentum
Stillness by the last breath.
Then, there is nothing, but hollowness and past.
The last breath-
That shuts the eastern window,
And silent present in bookshelf,
Depicts the history of melancholic effigy
Hanging on the walls.

DON'T CALL ME

When you call me
My breath stops
Warm blood stream flow down
And turn into an air balloon and fly
Away in the sky
Thousands of white doves spread their wings
In the endless meadow of heart
The spotless satisfaction lives on
And swing bemused.

When you call
I don't see any divisions in the sky-
I don't see any sun, moon, or stars
Or the mingling of the moonbeams
The whole sky then belongs to me
The cloud-covered body dazzle in festive silver.
Autumnal nights become sleeplessness

When you call
Oyster opens her shell in blessed pleasure
The Bestowed melancholy turns satisfaction

A bugle trill in mysterious sound from far ocean

That makes me drowned

And float over the broken waves

Please, don't call me that way

If you call

A solitary bird of my heart

Tries to touch the morning cauldron,

Crosses the boarder with a green pennon,

Dreams to savor the handkerchief

That wraps the blue heaven.

Please don't summon.

When it rains in the November night,

When the barge of intense emotions

Launch on reverse efflux of life.

You might not have strength to steer.

You might engage yourself

To the causeless and powerless

Damps for the fear of infamy.

Don't call me that way,

Please don't call me

I don't want to see a death and bald

Bird from your dossed eyes.

FIRE FACE

I sit with handful of fire
And observe, how can I endure!

The cave-dwellers invented
But didn't understand its intensive heat,
sharpness and severity,
How can it burn?
Everything is inferior to its virility.

It burns woods, cities, human beings and hearts
The last profound love, kingdom is also burned down
Fire changes new ruler on the throne
They rule past and present by fiery power.

I sit with the fire in hand,
Waiting to see fire transform stone into diamond.

WORSHIPER

I am not the worshiper of beauty
I am the worshiper of beautiful mind,
A beautiful poem impressed me instantly
Words from the heart are very appealing to me,
One page of pure thoughts keeps my spirits flourishing
A handful of aroma of dried flowers keeps me alive,
A piece of silent darkness gives me some serenity
I am not a worshiper of beauty.

INBUILT REFLECTION

From the braid of time
When one or two flower falls in a while,
I will not build an obstruction on the river
Making the garland of respect.
No, I'll not dampen the soils of poems
With the soft glands of women and breath
I'll not fill the empty granary with cutting
emotions into pieces –and
Shall not douse the darkness
by sacrificing the lamp and -
This time I will be an ancient peasant -
I'll cling some chins of stars on the folds
Of my spines, the stars that are waiting
for a thousand years.
Now I will be a lonely sailor for a distant destination
I'll attach the scent of the ocean on the wings.
I 've settled myself on my own reflection,
Because, in the end, what is true, what is love
Those are all your shadows, and this is life.

TODAY IS SPRING

It's still the wet nature with the tinge of winter
Green buds did not peep out
From the dry branches of oak tree,
Blue Jay did not didn't wake up from the
Lethargy of winter-sleep.
Still she opens her eyes and looked at the
Soft rays of morning sun
Robin spreads her wings silently on the incoming sign
What joy swing her bosom
Van Gogh's dust-covered colorful frame
Display abrupt exaltation
In the folds of solid ice cubes
Fine waves of refreshing stream flow
Somebody whispers on the stalk of un-bloomed Lilac
Today's spring; Windy silence make resonance
Today's spring in this wilderness of Diaspora.

THE CURTAIN WILL RISE

The regular stage-acting is on in the world stage
The hall was awakened by the dialogue,
The chandelier swing above
The struggle for existence is seen in finest style
Whisper and sounds of claps
The emotions are Prisoners behind the locked door
The shady heart mingles with light and shade
Wipes sweats on the arms of darkness
Nothing is stopped
Stage-show does not stop; the
blood oozes our from the legs!
Even then the curtain will rise! Darkness is in tunnel -
Still the curtain will rise! Fairytale hope enlivens -
On the last end of the tunnel
the little drop of light is seen!

EPISODE OF FOSSIL

While going to the sea, it was difficult
being trapped among the public
Then it takes the form separation, and
does not find the way.
Now the night and the days come in the same way
Diurnal transactions, regularly water droplets fall,
Clusters of silence eats up noon and nights.
It is difficult to move away from the center gradually
If it is more difficult if there is opposite
sense of attraction
Daily the lift goes up and
down, non-stop parallel journey
But despite all the movements,
something is very immobile -
As the dead man is standing,
The dead man gets open window
but did not see the sky
They do not have any hope and
have no expectation either
Look
While speaking about the dead

I lost myself into fossil story - or

am I talking about river?

In fact, if the river is bound, it does not remain rive.

[Translated by: Siddique Mahmudur Rahman]

DILARA HAFIZ

Date of Birth: 20 November 1955

Place of Birth: Manikgonj, Bangladesh

Education: PhD in Bangla Literature.

Publication: 11

Lives in: Toronto, Canada

E-mail: drdilarahafez@gmail.com

ADULT BOY

The boy that get much indulgence from the family
Have not get any practical
knowledge remain a greener
He is inadvertent and ungainly is his life style
His age grew up as if he didn't know how to walk
The boy is a sun-scorched soil
He didn't get the touch of soft mud
He is crumpled with injury and insult.
I've spread my loving hands to him
He caught hold of those with secured satisfaction
I lit in both of his eyes interest of life.

I stimulate him in art and culture, as much I could
The aged boy grows up in my attention – with interest
Lover and son, as if two rooms on a single house
As mother and beloved I move in both the rooms
When he returns shabby from his work-place
I clean him up with the water of solace and love
He grows up clinging to me, every day, the aged boy.

THE FIRST KODOM

Under the solitary mango grove
A lonely teenager forgetful
Kept her hand palm on her bosom
Her smoky breast didn't remain the same
Oh, look, its stone, gold ornament
She shrank in shame and with modesty
Her lonesome veil covered bosom,
As her crop-designed eyes shivered,
Her plump body startled at night.

The teenager woke up into a damsel, lady.

HIDDEN SIN IN THE LIPS

Had concealed wrongdoing on the lips
Burning on the forbiddingness
Returning the wrath.

The body is but Mahabharata
Unending play
All the seven chapters inside the body
The irritation of transformation

The complexity of art and body
Tension ridden
Falling in love at this age
The body got destroyed

Sin is hidden in the lips
Burning on the forbiddingness
Returns the wrath.

PRESENCE OF ILLUSION

Jumping out of the pot of illusion
This heavy body of my poem
Wanted to get a bit of shade under the tree of religion

I am the stubborn child of my father
Avoiding hundreds of obstacles of Veda and
overlooking Upanishad
Leaving away The Book of Tora, and even
The Bible, only that day I left
The green field of Quran and fled away

Someone spoke out 'Innallaha Ma-A-swabereen'
Nobody rushed to me with a Tasbih in hand
Any green island of solace did not rose up
Leaving out all the Ayats of sufferings
Even Zibrael or Michael
The 'Farista's did not ran towards me with
A few drops of waters of Rahmat in this earth

Like the fire of Namrud in the cool Milky Way
I uprooted with my scorched skin

An inexperienced before my heart alone
I'm alone like a ghost before my time
Destitute
Urchin!
Alone!

I LEARNT YOU ARE UNWELL

I learnt you are unwell
The one and a half-storied dwelling
That was brightly lit on the four sides of my dream
Shattered down just now
Suddenly the wind stopped blowing
The way the rippling of the stream stop
Sometimes the song breaks its melody
The way soft echo is not heard any more
When the large star breaks apart
The way the movement of the planet ends
 The aircraft breaks down on the mid air
The last hope of life stops abruptly
When an important bridge gives way
The way the moving traffic comes to an end
Or suddenly hearing the news of war breaks up
The life stream stops suddenly
Similarly, I became numbed
with death-fright struck me
I'm terrorized with earthquake
 I am now standing in this dreadful dark grave
Rescue me, it's still some time left

Spread the news quickly, that you are well
It might be a false news, like
our dreams we see at night.

AJIT PATRA

Date of Birth: 03 January 1971

Place of Birth: Jharkhand, India.

Education: Master of Hindi Literature.

Publication: 10

Lives in: Odisha, India

E-mail: ajit.writer@gmail.com

TURN OF THE ROAD

Road
You run straight-
Now take a turn to the right
The chirping of birds
Is heard from babul's branches
Crickets move in the paddy field.
I walk with my tragic voice
Along with the gloomy clouds.

Before me the Simili hills.
Here is Lulung
Where the trees on hills
Dazzle in torch light-like sunshine.

Now road is no more straight-
Turn to your right
In the sky of Ashadha's end
White patches of clouds hover
And the rain-soaked wind blows.......

I can get the smell of your heart.

Clouds wet with compassion
Move downwards.

I walk on and on
Leaving you far behind.

Sky is overcast with cloud
A plaintive Ashadha.
The road is no more straight-
Again, turn to the right
Flowers bloom on babul's branches.

The red road covered with moorum
This road has
Made me intoxicated
Your rhythm is in my voice .
No more the road
Now halt a little.

Thanks to geometry
You have given –
Proper shapes to
Angles , arms and lines

To the road.

I have again come back

To stand under the Karanja tree

The eyes

Wet with the rains

Of Ashadha's dense cloud,

Sunrays from behind

Fall on the mountain's face,

You laugh like the

Flowing water of the spring.

Again, I have come back.

In these days of Ashadha

With a cloudy heart.

Where else can I go

I am ever yours

I have come back to you.

IN THE HILL'S KINGDOM

Thread-like
Streams flow down
The Sinduri hills.

Down the hill-
Dust float in winter air
Where is water...?
Exhausted only in one crop field.
The hills stand as before
But without trees
Heard that an English sahib
Has taken away them all.

The festival of Pithachanka
Comes after makara.
The dubang Dance
Aluchop made of wheat
Sweet stalls....
The dance continues,
Shantal's Dubang Dance.

An eighty year
 old women
bend with age
begs on the way.
'Give me a rupee
I will have purchased a ladoo'.
With that single rupee
She will go back
To the fair
Through the hilly road
Only to eat the ladoo.

Nobody has given her a rupee
She has asked me
As she knew that I am a teacher.

Democracy is yet to arrive here.
Even if this kingdom is small
 it has escaped
The king's attention.

Democracy never
Reaches this place,

Only Laden comes here
Riding the ship of wealth!
Here Laden comes-
Mingling with the blood.

Where democracy does not rule
Laden comes
to this Hill's kingdom.

THE VILLAGE MARKET

The sons of the forest
Are coming down the hills
On the narrow roads of the hills
Santals and mundas carry
Bubei grass on their head and
Sal wood on their shoulder.
 Khadia sabar's basket
Is full of resin and honey.

Khadia sabra regularly goes to
Village market at Jugudihi.

Makara festival is not far off.
Red, blue and yellow clothes
Hang bellow the sal pulpit.

Carrot, cabbage, kurkuti
Vada, jalebi all have
Arrived for sale in the market.
Crowd swelling
In the market on the eve of makara.

At the entrance of the market

Bubei , timber, resin , honey

Everything entering the

Belly of the monster

Coins tinkling in saree's end.

A market places

For vending everything.

The moon roses

In the hills of village Amjharana.

All the monsters roared at a time.

These automobiles

Ran with their ten feet

Towards the town .

Moon-beam fell scattered on the ground

Also, the used saal leaves,

The murmur of the spring could be heard from a distance

...... the market place of the Jugudihi.

BABU COMES BACK IN ASADHA

The asadha….
Monsoon wind
Enters my window
Touches my body,
Goes deep and
Touches my heart.
On my bare body
The wind plays
With water drops
The sun-burnt body
Plays gleefully with asadha
In a celestial bliss.

Asadha's murmur
Flows slowly in my heart.
The earth is wet
Dampness engulfs me.
My mind is asadha's seeds
That I drop
On the fertile earth.
Tiny babu,

You have gone away
For some days
Leaving me alone.
The murmur of
Your half-years old
Feet, hands, fingers and face…
Everything is asadha for me

This asadha comes back
In my mind, in my heart.

FATHER'S STAIRCASE

Many times
I have climbed
Through my father's staircase
To reach my destination.
Whenever we wanted
It has helped us
To reach our place.

My father had built
This staircase by his hands.
This one is very old
Yet we use it easily
When required.
Yesterday I broke
That old staircase.
Covered with moss
Its plaster opens at places
Bricks visible,
The staircase looked dilapidated.
At mid-night
A strong wind blew

With heavy downpour.
Father appeared in my dream.
'where is my staircase?'
He asked in a whispering voice

I got up.
Standing on the veranda
I saw….
Everything washed away
In the dark of the rain.

I only uttered…
Father …… father.
Yes `Aju',
Even if you don't need
I could use that staircase
That would have
My last climbing.
What shall I do
With this new one.

In the morning I thought
In this world

All old staircases
Will fall down gradually.
Can we not build
A new staircase
Reserving the old one.

One day
I will also…..
If I come back
In a rainy night,
I would have
Gone up stepping in the air
instead of climbing
The new stairs.

PRISON OF BIGOTRY

Every chid
Is born in a prison
We spend each moment
In a prison,
In self-imprisonment

Day by day
I throw my-self
In to the dark depths of beliefs
More and more.

Bigotry
Is a deep dark prison?
From here no dreams
Of freedom can be seen.

To see the
Dreams of freedom
One has to break
The chains of bigotry.
Those girls,

Those cloud venders.
Living on both sides
Of the barbed wire
Can break the chains,
Those cloud vendors.

AFTER EVERYBODY'S WORK IS OVER

After everybody's work is over
I and my life.
This is the existence.
If I can write a poem
Does it harm you?

Water and mud
Fill Dharmtolla bus stand,
Sometimes gather inside the bus
Sometimes in village houses
Or in rain-soaked verandas.

Let the poem come anywhere
Does not matter much,
Even on the footpath-bed.
Sleeping on the footpath
'Jean' dreams of a beautiful world.

Nothing is at stake
It only exists in our mind,
Is our consciousness.

We are imprisoned is our
Own prisons
We also imprison others.

What harm is there
If I break the prison
After everybody's work is over?

For the sake of poetry
I can do this much.

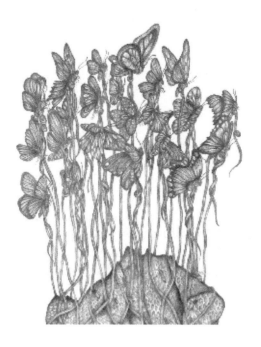

A WORLD WITHOUT PRISON

I dream of a
World without prison.

How will that
World look?

Perhaps a few animals
Have prisons apart from human beings.
But they fight for food and sex,
The way human beings
Behaved in ancient times.

If we can go back
To those primitive days.
No caste, no religion
No fight, no prison
Can we do that?

If suddenly
Flocks of aliens
Descend on the earth

And destroy the world
With wild fire
Can we protect our
Caste, religion
And boundaries?
I dream of flocks of aliens
I dream of wild fire
I dream of today's end
I dream of sunrise
Without prisons.

TINY FEET

Tiny feet
Daddy is coming.
Come.
I put on a
Pair of red shoes
On your feet,
At a distance
Our little child
Is walking
Holding his mother's hands.

Today
He holds books
In his hands.
Small town
Small wishes
Baba walks
Through dense mist
Through chilling cold
Through hot wind
Through dazzling tar.

Baba walks
Walks and walks
Runs and runs
The goal of job
Is far away.

Small town
Small wishes

Baba, a small child
What can I give,
Can I return
Those fairy tales
And those childhood days
When he was moving
Holding his father's hand
Days after days.

BARBED WIRE

Ceaseless rain

Drizzling throughout the day.

Has not the cloud girl

Been wounded

While returning to her homeland?

While crossing

The barbed wire

To go to alien country

Holding the hands

Of her parents,

Are the wings

Of the cloud-girl

Not hurt?

Does not the visa office

Pain her?

Even today for returning home

The barbed wire

Makes her bleed.

Rain… rain… Rain…

Uproot this barbed wire

If you fail

Oh, the cloud-girls,

Hold your hands

From both sides of the fence.

Your hands together

Will make the barbed wire disappear.

[Translated by Sangam Jena]

AKM ABDULLAH

Date of Birth: 1970

Place of birth: Sylhet, Bangladesh

Education: Bachelor of Arts

Publication: 06

Lives in: London, UK

Email: abdullah.20@hotmail. co.uk

WATER BIRD FAMILY

The river flows in our house. Torrential river.

Our family lives in the fold of this river waves.
Sometimes the fires of the river, fierce like the naval of
sea; and my mother used to burn the dishes in that fire.
And I used to- see the starflower, through the holes of
her wet saree.

There was no season in our world.

Even I never heard of climate

or word on clothes in our

family. Inside the half-broken wave of the river

mother kept the special organs of her female rights in
loops of strings as - pumpkin, which turn into seeds.

Sometimes the moon soaked my father's body with
borrowed fire; and he opens the pumpkin and starts
licking and eating as he liked.

The auditory tired waters wave, floated away the
broken mother's painful bones.

I can't remember these scenes anymore.
Instead, I forgot the former family

like floated water birds. And,
I forgot my past dwelling.

EVEN THEN, THERE WAS SHADOW

When the blood prices decrease in the world market, some people

cry out loudly. Some of them tarnish the blooming roses and decorate-

the reception room from the chest garden.

Even then, there was shadow.

Now, in folding of this shadow, our generations moved their hand and leg

like an over turned turtle. We're digitised. And our character continues selfied.

And, when the night is deeper, we sentiments like a blossomed lotus

and the feet of the rain we wear the gobbles; and sing joyously chorus:

''Oh! twists your waist -

Baby, twists your waist'' …

WATER SCRIPT

The dreams of my father's view – floating
away and my mother
sitting on the dam and picks up the pebbles of time –
from the water winnowing fan.
We down our knee - and on the water ceiling,
we keep the sigh of our lost family.

Some people drawn our faces on the wall
of silent water and with smile -

The open the door of night ...

And, we become products, instead.

FUGITIVE LIFE

...other side of the door, there is jasmine
tree and Inside the flowers too.
My mind blowing with
the fragrance of flower and fascinating like web.
The fugitive rats are immersed
to digging this life, from the birth-
And, one day the craving will stop
and darkness will cover the ground.

Then, I will stand up at the mysterious gate. A self-
autobiography will be swing on clay. After a world full
of surprise, there will be published of my life.

Oh!
One day, a flower bloomed in this universe. And I
loved that, for the value of my life.

STORY OF FOOLISH PEOPLE

Technically, a contaminated scarf wrapped
in our neck. We feel

drowsy and we start writing a standard
essay about animals, as you said.

Then we start thinking ourselves very wise.

When we sober up, and we start writing
again a quality essay about life;

the Composition became a story and main
character of the story exactly

match with your character.
At the end of the writing proofread, we see our
characters in this story are just as real as foolish people.

COLOURS OF BREATH

a.

The ridges of pond have lost from my chest pocket.
And the Madhabkunda waterfall is now within four by
six feet of my house.

I bathe and boat in this water.

b.

The place I live in this world; there is no sweet smell
like dense fog.

Now I am breathing the taste of blood and fires - to
live.

c.

When I stop the car at the traffic signals; I can see
through the windows', our people's walk in a dry face.
And I also looked at my mirror; I saw

a 'show smile' in my dry mouth.

But, every corner of the street, there are 'houses of worship' and inside - the festival of prayer.

MIDDLE-CLASS NIGHTS

The stables are inside the head. Someone open the gate.
Let the horses run in the middle-class field.
The field where the dark chews the people head
The field where the people silently licks the dark hips
where the people's silently commit to suicide.

Oh! someone stab that dark chest; like a wayward boy.
And let people listen -
the siren of the horse that came down from the head.

THE TIME

In my sitting room, I sit down watching television.
From the screen, tongue of my forefather's come out.
Someone cuts that tongue like
vegetables and pour into the bowl.

With the spoon of twentieth century; I
pick them up on my own bowl every day.

b.

Keep open your windows. I will send some moonlight
with slipped meteor and selfie stick.

c.

I decorated the evening twilight, because you are
coming.
After the long waiting; the thunder saws- cut the
waiting chest -
like the sky.

FORGETTING THE FASCINATED EDITORIAL

The flower is fell out
with conceit or committed suicide,
I could not take an interview of it.
The craving chapter of time, I
forgetting the fascinated editorial.

Now I am looking –
at the advertising column;
a tuberose and moon dialogue.

SIGH OF LUST

The light goes out of the skull and I drowned
into the deep darkness and
the fire of the time burns the heart.
Now I think myself as a wonder Refugee of the world.

At the late night, sleep flee from the eyes and
I keep on walking - on the high way -
I can see in the world chest, there is a jackfruit mess
Craving fly meeting on for whole night.
On the luxurious table, peperoni,
mushroom and tandoori topping pizza -
Ah! the smell of garlic sauce -
I wouldn't be surprised when see
a long procession of cockroach.

I have heard that diplomatic area
in the world are very safe;

Security surrounds.

But when I wish to I live there;

the fear grown up in the soil box and

cheerfully slaps on the cheek of life.

NAZMUN NAHAR

Date of Birth: 01 January

Place of Birth: Chittagong, Bangladesh

Education: Master of Business Administration

Publication: 03

Lives in: Sydney, Australia

Email: nazu1971@gmail.com

LAST DAY

If you give the advice to go to war
By the time I discarded my eyes
Threw away my cupboard
Soiled Handkerchief,
And Salt-caller –

On the last day of the reception
We walked together
When all our legs are next to the wire
Our blind eyes are on the paddle of the rickshaw -

It's important to be our separation
As it is important to love together!!
By our own scratch
Heart became sliced-
Ah! there is nothing else -

But on the last day
The day of floating in the ocean,
Leaving behind the barrack
That day just a bitter of wine

Made of neem leaves

Affliction the death of the body

Same as our open doors and

Windows wide open

Ah!! The last day

Now every day is our last day!!

I 'M YOUR GRIEF

There was uncultivated land
And those green grass
Along the lonely road
I knew on that day
I was a sleepless traveler -

But listen carefully
I tell you
The shirt gets wet, buttoned up
There rises a cloudy noon
In deepest eyes –

There's no one anywhere
Just I understand
I am your grief-

YOU'RE A KNOWLEDGEABLE BOY

When you just stand like a king
Your bosom is just as high as the sky
And when you became a wise bright guy

When an ocean came to your feet
I became air of piano
Harmonious blue notes
In my sorrow -

Oh, my cloud hero
Silently just become a deer
And I want to be a green forest

A white house in a deep wilderness
In its big deepest pond, I will bath
And spend evening, noon and night
I will make your black night
Into a bright noon for you
Ah! For long time there was no rain in that planet!!

BIRD LIFE

While crossing the road, I lay down on the zebra crossing.

Three cars looked on my bosom and saw three birds were sitting on my heart.

And then they knew the history of me

I was a bird in my early life –

Burning in the cloud

I just reclaimed on the sky

I saw your rolling life.

Crossing the border with the meandering train

You just stuck in the middle of the river.

When the bird flew away I caught its wings.

But why you are crying

Making all the passer-by standing.

THANKFUL TO GOD

At midnight I felt pain in my heart
and understood
It has been eight days since I died Before some
moments of your death –

When you put your feet on the paddle of cycle
I just told you death is like a receiver–
It will never stop -

Emotion ups and downs with Sufi songs tunes
Sunlight of the sun and cotton are of ropes brooded on
our graves –

We just said remembering the words of God
Oh God! We have not any Ingratitude to you
Again, forgive us for once
And send to us lots of love –

STAY THERE

One day the city will know
We both were Geist-
In the game of love
We left the salt of our heart to the ocean
Kept our eyes on eyes and said
Love you, honey.
We crossed the dark night
Call it beyond the time
'Actually, all was false of us '
The rocks that are on stone-bush
Stood in the stairs with little bit smile '
Seeing him in art-theatre
Oh! It is time to come
The wraith does not have any night nor day
Though our cat life –
One day when we were
Walking together in the deep forest
A boy made a snapshot of us
And lost in rain –
He told –
Oh, stay there –
You better stay there!!

TAKE ME UP, O LORD

I will give all my endurance to God
In the endless space, I am just a worm!

Oh, God! Please open all the windows and doors
The scarf of the queen and the scent
tree became wet before Noon-

Drops of water and the hair of Shakuntala
in the shower room, everything going
under shrub –
Please let me sit on your dear Borak
I am just dying in the fire of Ginsberg and wine
Oh God! please take me up to you!!

IN DARK AND LIGHT

The shirt was hanging on devoid

And rolling to the cave of light –

It rolling to land, lie down on grass,

then became water –

I went back to the shirt.

Though I am a cactus of Jupiter of ancient time–

And once I was a human being –

But I came back to a wood and lie down

under a primitive tree

And saw my Almighty --

Ah – So polite passionate my Creator is

There is a round cold moon in his hand –

A gentle breeze blowing at me

And threw to the sky--

I whispered to my Creator

Would you tell me–

How many Gods live in this locality?

FOURTH GENERATION

In one evening of March, you sat on
a Hara-kiri valley and thought –
The sadness of losing love, would
not relieve by any ointment
So, brother and sisters –just gather under the flag
Eat raw meat and say, 'we all express solidarity '
And hide the prostitute under the wings of a bird –

And the men who adore their God –
let them do worship to forth breast of his women
and the woman who lost her respect in a fast vehicle.
The nude orange which is floating on ozone
they would say from women and men
a new Alien will be born –
They are our fourth generation.

DISSOLVING

This city is dissolving into my body

I am melting into the city

I'm walking,

Devouring

And I'm cleaning my wounds with my spits

You're laughing turning into ten in the mesosphere

Traversing the mist your ten multiply into hundred

The road, this city has turned into you

You've drawn a circle

I'm the core

Touching the circumference

I'm walking, diluting, returning to the parameter

I run from the center to the fringe

When I want to permeate

Hundreds of you resist me with barricades.

You eat on me

you clamber after you're full

You sit on my body

You place a chain on my back

And sit at ease

Lit a cigar and puff out smoke
Make out a circle with the smoke
You relax with ease and comfort
And bellow out like a gander.
Ahh!

SAKIF ISLAM

Date of Birth: January 18

Place of Birth: Dhaka

Education: MBBS

Publication: 01

Lives in: Virginia, USA

Email: sakifi147@gmail.com

SHATTERED MOONRISE

Our love was like the spring flowers blooming
Amid the stipples of dragonflies looming.
Like the sacred snows of winters, no more
We were lost in a time we never knew before.

How I longed to be at your side;
To cradle you softly as you cried,
To bathe ourselves in laughter and mirth,
Forgetting our shadows, it's price and worth.

How I loved to caress your skin
To fade the hate residing within.
Just knowing that I was there with you
Lit up my world of black and blue.

But like the marvel of the sun at dawn
Our happiness was abruptly gone.
Fate took you away with faint goodbyes
And left me under a shattered moonrise.

FEATHERS FROM HER BROKEN WINGS

The sun rose high and the clouds gave away
Skies wept at the sight of celestial decay.
The moon gave sighs and the stars did sway
The colors of the world to turn into gray

What happens when the light you
wished upon fades to nothing
And crawls into the darkness
from which you were running?
Feathers from her broken wings hovering before you
Making you question every belief that you swore to.

Dusk and dawn are all but gone
And the line in between is vaguely drawn.
Eyes can't close for the tears must flow,
The tears can't flow for the eyes don't know.
The eyes don't know what the mind never sees,
So, in reality it's the heart that forever bleeds.

THIN GRAY LINE

Sleep reduced to naps
Meals reduced to snacks
Dreams reduced to that thin gray
line between the black.
Silence of nights tainted
By voices reacquainted
From the fibers of a time left behind
by those who made it.
Sickness lingers cold and wet
Mistakes of old beget regrets
Falling from frowning eyes that
try but are cursed unable to forget.
Like a moth to the flame
I'm enthralled by the pain
I'm lost in the rain of all the hostility and shame.
The world is a sick place
Words full of disgrace
Swallowing the pride won't get rid of this taste.
And life is a quick race
Nights come and kill days
Skies part even if you don't fix your mistakes.

THE NARRATIVE THAT ECHOES

Piano keys hammer the stings of the heart.
Notes and rhythms are eruptions and waves
Of blood and thoughts, emotions betray
The senses of the body, but time never waits.
It creeps by like a cursed cat crossing your path.
You hesitate for a second but you never fully stop,
Because we are unstoppable, but stand back
When we see fire and bullets
and barbed wires and shootings
And hear the cries of home but
we keep going and going.
When our shattered jaws hang like broken doors
And we can't scream anymore, we finally stop to listen.
Clarity, only when we've stopped the self-delusional
Narrative that echoes through our actions or prison.
But by then we've scorched the
earth with our flaming bodies
And our hands might as well be feet slowly rotting,
Because all we can do is stand still on all fours
Like dogs sentenced to be put down forever more.
Too late to reach out for salvation;

No heaven or hell, just a state of damnation.

FLEE WITH THY FEATHERS

My heart aches, and a drowsy numbness pains

My sense, as though of hemlock I had drunk.

Blood seems to cease flowing through my veins;

Within the earthly poisons my heart has slowly sunk.

Your ghastly song taunts my soul

And thy presence alone haunts my world.

Your smile of joy, though loved it was,

Suffers me, knowing not what it does.

So sweet it would be if your song was gone;

Such a silence I wait for at the break of dawn.

Take upon your wings my misery and sorrow,

Flee with thy feathers before I wake tomorrow.

Pull thy cancerous beak out of my heart,

Let it beat once more, as it did in the start.

Unearth those talons from the core of my being

And undo the blindness my eyes keep seeing.

Release me from the shadows you have cast,
Fly back into the cage buried deep in my past.
End thy unwarranted perch upon my bones,
Once wrapped in flesh, now wrapped in stones.

The blossoming nest that you lovingly built
Fell to pieces as your love began to wilt.
Though you were the flame that caused me to burn,
You I still long for, for you I still yearn.

SAD TO SAY

It's sad to say it all ends today
Because what we built you threw away.
You left my world with a gaping hole;
Now stranded, broken, I wait alone
On a tear-stained way you left me standing.
Left me gasping, left me panting,
Left me asking why you closed the casket.
Was it the screaming? I thought we passed it.
Was I just dreaming or did you just mask it?
You hear me pleading, my eyes are bleeding
Watching this rope hanging from the ceiling;
No more grieving and no more breathing.
Don't turn back if you plan on leaving.
Because today the man you knew will depart
Take a good look as he hangs his heart.
It's sad to say I won't make it on my own
But at least today I won't be alone.

LAST LULLABY

You are my lucky rabbit's foot
My golden horse shoes
My only lucky charm.
Like an addict I'll forever run towards you
Like light from a dying star.
You are my last lullaby
My lover from another life.
My favorite song
Never skips a beat.
My source of strength
But for you I'm weak.
I give you my word
Unbreakable, unlike promises
To give you my world
And shield you from the awfulness.
In days to come I might forget
When we're gray of different shades.
But there is nothing I will regret
As long that wicked smile never fades.

PRAYERLESS

Show me what love is beyond the line that

Divides and conquers; the lines that blind us.

I bask in the lonely nights

When the only lights are the bright of your eyes

Just enough to give me sight.

But the hues of the moonlight

Seem so dark and empty,

Where shadows assume life

And plot to end me.

The claws of guilt creep and move like

God just left me; not so friendly.

Why did you leave me by my lonesome?

Didn't want much but for memories to not haunt us.

Sitting on the staircase, defeated and prayer less,

I see my life fade away but I couldn't care less.

Who do I to blame for this?

ROWNAK AFROZ

Date of Birth: 14 August

Place of Birth: Dinajpur, Bangladesh

Education: Doctor of Medicine

Publication: 02

Lives in: Ohio, USA

Email: papeea@yahoo.com

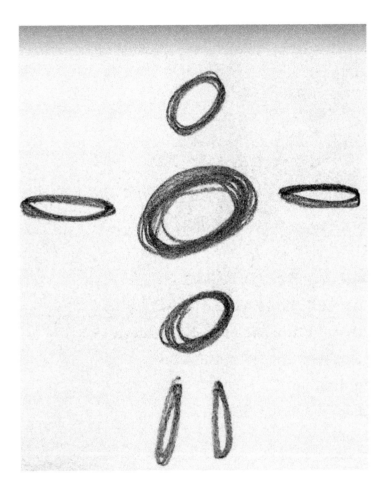

DANCE

In a crowd of clouds, I danced to classical beats.

Invited the birds; with me they will stay.

Asked the moon to make music with her tarboulin.

She too agreed; her Bhairavi she did play.

NEIGHBORHOOD

On and above the far horizon
Floats the magnanimous sky.
Pinnacles of the mountain range
Holding it high.

The gleaming river beneath
Caresses the ripples in synchronicity,
Plays a loving sonata
If not symphony.

LOVE AND DEATH

I could sing, I could dance
If I wanted to, I could fly
Beyond the universe.
Yet, I chose to kneel
Before my passionate love,
Get hurt, bruised, bleed, and die.

When the despondency of dusk sets
The soul shivers and screams
And doesn't let go of memories,
Intense and soaked in bluish pain,
Once thought to be ethereal
But made to look utterly ugly.
That very non-celestial moment,
The dream, shatters in vain.
There's the problem, I am dying.
So I mourn my own death,
Repent in owe and anguish,
As my soul flies eternally.

A LONELY WALK

This road is pebbled.

The one adjacent, full of thorny vines.

It is deep, dark, and tortuous.

My wings are tired

And feel like stones.

The dimming daylight engulfs my senses.

The mountains turn blue,

The valleys, brown and barren,

Trigger confusion.

Yet, I must reach the end

Alone.

LIVING WITH SOLITUDE

Since you have gone
I am befallen, alone.
A lonely moon
Drifts through a bleak sky
Seeking its own horizon.
The fresh jasmine
On my balcony loses fragrance.
So many long days without you.
What kind of life is this?

In the solitude
Of our lover's chamber
My eyes are heavy, yet sleepless.
I am exhausted, dazed, dreamless.
You left with no word of your return
And I already long for you.
Amongst crowds of countless people moving on
I am desolate, alone.
What kind of life is this?

A DAY IN DESPAIR

An overcast sky,
Not even a glimpse of light
To shear through the compact cloud.
A dreary landscape,
Wild trees, tall and old, with bare branches
And the mountain, barren,
Longing for rain.
I look through the window
And there he is!
A blind man walking
With his white cane,
His faithful dog pulling
The master by the leash,
Rustling the dry leaves.
A monstrous emptiness
Engulfs my senses.
The man doesn't know
The difference between day and night
And here I complain
About faint day light.
What a lost mind, what a shame.

LIVE AND LET LIVE

Life is a boat
Sailing through the roaring waves,
With sharks in the waters
And skies dark with clouds.
Sometimes sailing alone
In the middle of no where
And no lighthouse in sight.
Living is still worthwhile
And beautiful.

Let's help wipe some tears,
Hold tight a sick, trembling hand,
Shine light to tired, lost eyes,
Treat a painful wound with care.
If you can, catch a falling bird.

One step at a time
A long path is paved.
Touch one life at a time with such grace.
I assure you,
An enormous difference is made.

Let's fill the boat
Until we anchor
To the unknown shore,
With blessings and love
To nourish our soul.
Living is worthwhile
And life is wonderful.

THE SUN MUST REAPPEAR

The music must go on
The marching shouldn't stop
Forget the fallen past
Don't let your spirit drop.
Let the dark cloud move out
It's bound to float away, or shower
Magic has to happen
The sun must reappear!

With sunlight the river sparkles.
Green grows greener.
Our hearts leap in elation.
Birds fly happily and higher.
We must find the lost words,
Stop mourning,
And change the black gear.
Let's chase our dreams and dance.
Poetry must reappear.

LEAVING BEHIND

I left my stories in songs of the rippling river,
In the autumn dew
Drenching the paddies
I left my tears.

Dancing lights all across the sky,
The fluttering butterflies with shivering wings.
I left my dreams
In the hearts of fragrant roses.

There will be a night
Bathed in moonlight,
You'll look around,
But I'll be no where to be found.

Don't stare at the sky,
Don't hope and cry
The sullen star
That fell silently from the heavens
Shall never return there.

MY SELF-INDULGENCE

In the kingdom of my own spirit, I am the sole Queen.

I am the subject, only one, none else exists there at all.

This long singleness has matched me so nicely,

It wraps me always, like how my favorite
undergarment fits,

Singleness clothes me well, keeps me totally splendid.

In the vacant shores of my heart,

I notice the return of seafarers,

Sailors laying anchors at the end

of an exhausting voyage.

And, sitting afar, I observe their frequent movements.

There in the middle of foamy waves,

I observe the appeal of interlude

to the real game of parting.

Yet, I hold strongly to my belief made

within the folds of my palm.

This singleness has its own wealth, its own richness.

Its own internal joy is plenty,

Its own horizon of unbreakable love.

Its own game of hide-and-seek between

Sun and Moon in the tidy sky.

So, all of you, please return.

I don't desire any gifts from you, nor any praise.

I prefer to converse freely, alone with my own shadow.

I don't expect any uncalled strolling

of any wayfarer, dweller, or guest

Inside the kingdom of my own spirit.

LALON NOOR

Date of Birth: June 30, 1973

Place of Birth: Thakurgaon, Bangladesh

Education: Master of Bangla Literature

Publication: None

Lives in: Ohio, USA

Email: lalon_noor@yahoo.com

GHOST SEASON

You're a presenter, biased, me too a known goblin recites name of Ram non-stop. Exchanging the expertise of the arrange a round-table meeting in the balcony of peace-lodge, a smiling politician.

It's being a season of gnomes, afternoon of kites, top-days the rains of blood pours down in the country, this year the red-rose breeding will be good – die to printing mistake, this news gets big coverage in the sleeping newspapers, and looking at the eyed-Neem tree, the mourning was relieved by the ghosts sitting on the stage, by consuming burp of satisfaction.

Sitting on the floating alluring electric wires, the smiling bats know blind can see everything, but the eyed person can see nothing at all.

POLITICS

During the time of providing comfort
I felt desire of flying
With dug dugi in hand, I clap,
'Here children, call out,
Hurray, hurray.......'

Now listen
I sell remedy of all the diseases
Complex and chronic.

If non-responsive, the price is returned
But you'll never find me again.

WELLBEING OF SUN RAYS, SONGS OF WAR

Duck gets happy to see the water in the pond, the electric nets spread in gluttony of prey. So, the song of war days is played suddenly, safe hands of frolicking kid.

Among these the sun rays were exchanged among the water and

 bird on subject of pathos. Here, a few known white storks with their beloved product and commodities hid themselves into red-colored breast-pocket in fear of firing. When loving teals flew to the west, the day dawned with eastern wind, the year is Seventy-One. Leaving aside all these incidents the stars break the silence, wellbeing of sun rays.

THIS SLEEP, THE SLUMBER CYCLE

This sleep slumber cycle; roaming around
I collected those fig-character, mimosa pudica shrub.

In the class of Political Science show
out any posture, any joke
They make you dance in any ring or intrigue.

AS if easy flow of blood stream
is coming out of husking mill-
Such profound crimson color is not
seen in flowers and paint brush
The quantity you could hold in your posture.

Still sleep, that slumber
Is circling, in cyclic order- up and down
I embrace the fig-character,
You're fiery mimosa pudica shrub

THE PICTURE

This is a brilliant and dazzling close picture
Colorful, flickering and sharp picture
Grinning smiling pitched picture
Squint-eyed portrait very good picture
Taken in mid-shot close three-quarter picture
Inner from the camera's frame is the picture
Of a man.

One-fourth of the picture is in long-shot
The picture is out of the frame of the camera
Of animals.

[Translated by Siddique Mahmud]

RIPA NOOR

Date of Birth: January 23, 1973

Place of Birth: Rangpur, Bangladesh

Education: Master of Bangla Literature

Publication: None

Lives in: Ohio, USA

Email: lalon_noor@yahoo.com

WOMAN, FLOWER AND RAYS

O woman, O sky today touch flowers
Didn't you look at border line, not the error

This flower bloom everyday poetry is its light
Men covers those all the defaults

All the memories of souvenirs in the lives
All become illuminated with women's lights

I've seen some bizarre in the rays
A black shadow of weird shape calls out

Here which unknown hands covers the sun
Search for this path night in broad day light

It's not a night, a well-known shadow
Remove that and see the charm of life.

THAT DAY ONE DAY

That day	There was police and a man
That day	There was sufferings
That day	Love is lost
That day	There was wound in the heart

That day one day is clear

There was love in this heart

That love was intense.

I'M TOO A RIVER

I'm too a river

The waves are dreams, dream is mine

One

By one

I clean the darkness in the dark.

In the prayer of love

I bring peace

Not in power

In the ocean like river.

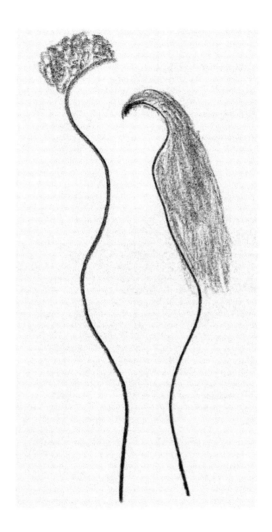

FLOWER BLOOM ALL OVER THE GARDEN

The sun shines on the garden its
time to flower to bloom,
The garden grabbed the mind,
the heart binds in debt of love

I fly as her evening birds,
Spread my wings and collect flowers
floating with the wind, like kites.

I roam around the flower garden, with
a reel of thread in my hand,
Flower damsel, flower nectar,
the birds fly on the flowers

I look for her flowers at the night of Falgun
Flowers bloom all o'er the garden
the flowers are her capital.

GREENISH FRAGRANCE IN MOONLIGHT

Now you're not the guest, sowing

seeds in your own chat

Like well-kept Sonnet, its sonnet

to get afraid in the evening on this earth.

There are no rotten ideas in the random meeting

In the meet, I look for green

fragrance is lying in the moon beam

By soling the mysteries, the map

turn out to be gun powder

Talent of blood; living memories of Bengal

So, geography in history, geography

in map and map in green.

Suddenly the reflection of the existence

is seen still in the evening,

The scent of green is expressed in the alphabet

Still, the spectrum of senses brings

breathtaking map of the world today.

[Translated by Siddique Mahmud]

SHAMIM AZAD

Date of birth: 11 November 1951

Place of birth: Mymensingh, Bangladesh

Publications: 35

Education: Master of Bangla Literature

Lives in: London, United Kingdom

Email: lekhok@gmail.com

LAY TO REST

To bury or not to bury the bard's complete works,
To be or not to be, is no more a question to me.

His work, a wise lumbering elephant
weighing me down, as I push him
up translation's steps.
His greedy words are like a swarm of mosquitoes -
have sucked my blood, worn me out -
I cannot imbibe this multifarious mountain no more!

Let's bury them all, have fish and chips, and go home.

Though I am aware of why my words
rendered the sky like arrows.
Why Mohammed Ali was compared
as a Shakespeare in the boxing ring,
Mandela lasted 27 years in prison valiant as one
who tasted death once,
and why Charlie Chaplin wanted to play as Hamlets!
It is because, his name is good
for grace, commerce and dominance.

Nevertheless, I was petrified of him and still I am
When I dress his charismatic characters
in Bengali attire -
swap his doublet for a dazzling Sherwani,
a ruff for a readymade Urna, and a jerkin for a jama.
I shiver with worry -
Will I lose his semantic ambiguity of the text?
Have exhausted it, burnt the texture?

Mr. Shakespeare, your words are
like the witches in your Scottish play
who say one thing with one word
when they mean other,
which, more often than not leads to more murders.
Your intricate English verses makes me feel,
what is lost between your words and mine, were you!
I sense the challenges in my bones,
trauma and tension in my hair roots,
I hear rattling noise of my vertebra and
you consume my calm.

While you did not speak a word in four hundred years,

we the translators perhaps spoken more than you ever
assumed!

Surely, digging the resting carcass,

to make room for his bones to be arrested forever,

and to lay to rest did not work.

Let us start his funeral,

sprinkle golap jol on the ground,

pour some pure ghee in it,

burn his complete works as we step into the new year.

Let's bury the ashes, plant our seeds to grow,

in the land of myths of William Shakespeare.

EMPTINESS IS...

When you wake up
early in the morning
In your burrow
With your eyes shut
Your fingers, hands, arms,
body, mind and soul
Extend.
They grow and stretch
like they never did
They search and look
for a touch desperately
But return without.
Ah...

IN THE SILENCE

I hear my eye

lashes are dropping

the barks are cracking

the blue bells are chattering with the long lustrous grass.

I hear the whispers of insane insects

over the ripening raspberries'

made up of many juicy globes drupelets.

In delusion, in the silence.

THE GRENFELL TOWER

A fire has its own smell,
a distinctive story.
Silver birch or aspen wood,
lovely lavender or a victory.

Grenfell Tower
did not smell of that, however.
It smelt of pee soaked nappies,
mothers' milk and burnt breasts
plastic brushes tangled with fallen hair,
deformed leather furniture
a whirling clay-cloud and dark air.

Grenfell Tower's heat,
sharp blades with thousands of eyes
an enormous body
a barbecued human head.

Breathless carbon thick
from scorched certificates
of English as second language,

undistributed wedding invitations,

burnt chip wheel-chair.

In the sky layers-

of poisoned black soft fat

sat still, there.

Only few hours ago

they had body and bones,

a music of their own.

FRUIT WOMEN

(after the painting 'Running Plum Man' by Salvador
Dali)

Tell me woman how you hold
Those fantastic fresh fruits
On your lips,
In your bare hands
In your fingertips,
On your back bones.

You hang it on hangers of your body
To dry in the sun and store
For rainy days for your family
So they can sustain the crisis, restore
Their energy and
Don't need to go door to door.

You have a hidden harvest
Prickly, spiky and blunt
They come out
When men are in trouble
And when they want.

Some of your fruits
Have the texture of anger;
A ravishing spicy smell;
A special power to ignite,
But only few people can tell.

When they know it
They raise their eyebrows
Think it's outrageous and odd
An anomaly in their house.

Women, you are running with fruits
Without proper clothes and shoes,
Bare hands, half fed or with an empty stomach
While you continue and produce.

Your fruits are your busy breasts,
Filled with the juice of life inside,
But your curious brain
Has fruits of fire and flame.
Women, why don't you confide!

GAZA

There was a time...
The roses grew
smelt lovely smell of incredible infants
and the moisture reached air laid next to them
the colourful roses sang
suereal syrup filled cups of summer drinks.
Real roses hanged in thewindows
in doors and in the couryeards in Gaza
in the life of the people over there
They had births weddings, meetings, majestic nights
delightful dawns lasting fare well long to remember.

Now in the same good old garden
they have a growing warfare
sparking gun powder bursts like fearful flowers
it has become invincible
hey, we the world people,
do we really care

TREPIDATION

I did not watch the video;
Kept both eyes shut tight.
Yet still,
With my sister's soaring,
My bravery abandoning,
The grass grew greener
On my dying skin.

Fear is winning.
Fear is getting more work.
Fear is the coming back from
Under tons and tons of concrete,
deposited;
Fright is her name.
She is my twin;
A twin who is alive and active.

I have lived with her since
Our senses arrived,
Because she is my sister.
I have lived with her like

A life with terrible toothache.
She has shown me the dull,
Dried, fried and black blood.

My mother's face
Like burnt old leather purse.
My runaway father ran,
Never phoned us back.
I had to breathe with her,
Because she is my sister.

I can hear the bruised past.
1971 is whispering,
Telling me:
Fear is just waiting for me
To win again,
Because I am her sister.
Shutting my eyes,
Closing up my ears,
Did not stop her return.
It never does.

Sitting on a weathered wooden bench

in an autumn park I feel
there must be some yellow leaves
still hanging on few strong branches around.
And the branches are trying to streak them down,
divorce them once for all and forever.

ALTAB ALI

He cooks tea with loads of sugar,
he loves watching wrestling at the Albert Hall,
lightings at Christmas, in Trafalgar Square.
He cooks curry with finely
chopped fresh green coriander
and he listens to Baul songs on an old tape-recorder.

Altab Ali, an ordinary Bangladeshi factory labour,
works in a bleak Hanbury Street basement,
producing coats of leather.
He came across the seven seas and thirteen rivers,
to make a fortune for his family living in Sylhet
by the mighty Monu Gang river.

His bendy Bibi was a great storyteller.
'People can be loved and respected
regardless who they are',
said his grandmother.
So, he thinks, anyone can make
his home in an unknown city
if one doesn't hold animosity against another.

The vendors at east London's Petticoat Lane market
make him feel he is not an anomaly, not an intruder.

He loves his jungle-printed half sleeved shirt
filled with smells moth-balls from Sylhet – Zindabazar.
It can be washed by hand with soap and water,
can be hanged to dry by the burning radiator,
and he can wear it without ironing
because it is made of polyester.

He is fearless and perhaps a little bit careless
and think people cannot simply murder
just because you are different from them, dissimilar.
So he never feared dark places and white faces,
and walks home after work without any fear.

But when he was attacked by a racist male,
near the street called Adler.
he was so surprised that he dropped his tiffin carrier
and swallowed piercing punches.
When he couldn't take any more
he cried for help.

Before his sky got saffron red
before his body had a last quiver
he desperately wished he was there
by his childhood Monu Gang river.
But no one came and he died
on the crushed sycamore on the grass of St Mary's
and they sucked his blood forever.

And next day Altab Ali became
a news item for a BBC reporter.

BARGAIN
(to József Attila)

Goodbye József
I'm leaving –
Cutting through the metallic Danube
Piercing through Jibril's rays of light
That smells so of combustion –
For that copper-coloured Bengal
Floating off in sunlight

Now
On Andrassy Street
My evening sari will leave no trace
In the folds of water-wrung cloud.
Decay in this brown skin,
Newly-sprouted body hair
Or sudden alarm in a dream –
These you will no longer sense,
Nor the trace of a new poet
In this city where you are
The supreme one

This is your city
Where gothic earth & piers,
Medicine fountain & smell of carbon,
Fatigue solidified as granite
With my hair's mask left there

swished
And my intimate clothing, love,
I'm leaving all this, along with
My senseless poems

This Christ-yellow dawn
This symphony of Margaret Island
The body-bread that is of this city
I am taking with me &
The heart of these stone eggs,
This red-showing sweet rain.
Apart from this –
From today you'll turn into a piece
Of derelict unfruitful land
A sperm-less pot
A paper goulash.

So, tell me,

Do you want this back again?

Words wound round with cellophane

Words steamed together by my emotion

Or your jaundice?

Don't you know that you fathered them!

[translated by Shamim Azad & Stephen Watts]

THE MOST BEAUTIFUL SWEET THING

I live where
the world's most excellent fruits
and most respectable people are and
where the most beautiful birds build their nests.

Vulgar people live here too,
in filthy ditches brilliant water lilies bloom.
The smell of children's pee-soaked blankets
        surrounds the place,
and I live here, too, as excess.

I am the citizen of an extremely populated country:
everything in it drowns at times
                in the floodtide of the new moon.
Sometimes the swan's neck emerges from the lava
                    stream glistening in the sun.
The dream pitcher doesn't wait here for a touch
                but simply floats away –
With such countless disgrace unbearable wounds
and pain
under the merciless gaze of the developed world

I live in this country like this.

Because the world's most amazing fruits
                have grown here,
the most respectable people,
                the most beautiful birds,
I survive through the year, through rain and shine –
I survive with the indomitable longing
for the harvest's golden grains
in this place, like this.

**[translated by Syed Manzoorul Islam & Carolyne Wright
with the poet]**

ZAKIR HOSSAIN

Date of Birth: 16 December

Place of Birth: Dhaka, Bangladesh

Education: Bachelor of Arts

Publication: 04

Lives in Singapore

Email: zakir.journal@gmail.com

NATURE

Like you, at times
when grief pours down on me,
nothing can ease the pain but
Nature,
an enchanting touch of magician.

While you enjoy the sunshine
and sea waves in beach,
angle (for fish) at green riverbanks,
and enjoy the gardens,
sweet shelters of trees,
I immerse myself in noise of gigantic machines.

For me Nature is,
the soil soaked in
sweat of craftsmanship,
that streams down every moment
through every inch of my skin.

And, in the tea breaks shorter than a glimpse,
I sail through the pages of poetry

in search of the peace.

Still at times,

when grief pours down on fatigue-torn me,

in roads and in MRTs

I behold the faces of the infants,

free and pure as Nature would be.

I AM SORRY

Sorry, I am sorry,
for hanging on your spotless wall
this painting, mere strokes of colour

Don't worry,
I'll take it down right away

The subject of this painting:
Life in exile
Name:
The happy bird
(A beloved's endearment
for a migrant worker)

To the right after the crossroads
and there you are at the cluster of households
the fun-filled playgrounds of the child
and that green patch you see
moving from opaque to light
the half-hearted lights that become yellow
spread out to the plane

From here begins the caress of the brush
that has dissolved slowly
into the smoky brass of the sky
To the left lies diffused the abir-covered evening
standing still at the doors of the stars

Excellent, says the rain
and showers its many greetings

An old man stands
close to the painting
and says in a moist voice:
The whole canvas dyed
in the tired eyes
of innumerable workers
Unloved faces
and the poetic biography
that grows around stories of faded dreams
their grotesque domestic furniture
the pollen of love, beyond touch
the fading signs of a kiss

Some people from the crowd said:

Craftsman of civilization

this world will bow before you in gratitude

forever

Embarrassed

I am removing the picture

and again I say sorry

I am very sorry.

BIRDS FLYING

People walks around, I draw their footsteps sincerely

Footsteps seems like their faces,
in many shapes and impressions
And then, all on a sudden
I found a beautiful pair of footsteps,
Oh, how beautiful they are!
I rise my eyes to see them
I have found my mother and father,
I bowed down and kissed their feet,
Mother took me to her arms and
kissed me on my forehead
Said, flowers may blossom on your every word
My dad kissed on my hand and said,
And those flowers may have the scent of your mother.

My mother's name is Amirunnesa,
Mossammat Amirunnesa
Whenever father called her, Amirun … Amirun …

I can hear I birds flying around the house.

RETURN TO THE RIVER

I go to river to cure the disease of watching people
And still I see them in the excitement of it — in its
melodious song.

I stare at the faces
Joy, pain, horror, hardworking, amateur, fool, greedy,
innocent, shy, ridiculous, frustrated, tired, hopeful
I wonder how many faces they have!

I learn to make the mask from them
I sell them in the market, in the bank of the river
And people buy only those happy marks
And rest of the masks remain
unsold — I use them sometimes.

And then some creatures look like human, come and
Buy all the unhappy masks
And the next year, no happy faced mask they bought,
They want some animal face.
But I could only make the human mask.

Animals, do you have any masks, too?
An animal faced procession comes
Pass across me, giving some sweetmeats
I ate them and return to the river.

ZEBRA CROSSING

In a happy spring day, in the afternoon
Someone came and said, let's fly to another state
I agreed nodding my head.

I flew to another country, and
I can't breathe sometimes
And then I wish to watch people again
I stand beside some zebra crossing
I heard that so many people come and go

And I watch them walking, in their fancy dresses
I look at their faces, their footsteps
But can't find anyone inside of them.

Beside a lifeless wall
I write down these day by day

Under the sun or in the rain
Flowers blossom on them
and the scent of those flowers
Flows all over the city,

I see, someone wrote POET beside my name

I remain quiet

Standing beside the zebra crossing

In a hope watch human kind.

SUJAN BARUA SAIM

Date of Birth: 10 December

Place of Birth: Chittagong, Bangladesh.

Education: Doctor of Medicine

Publication: 03

Lives in Ohio, USA.

Email: nyusmle@yahoo.com

BESIDE THE RIVER OF HAPPINESS

Who is the refugee today?
Who comes to whom, and who departs?
Still the wall of hatred grows up along with prayer
The hundreds of artworks of disintegration!

Who 're you, sits on Peacock-throne?
Smiling like a demon; On the green valley
The birds covered their beaks with crimson kerchief

Some intoxicated devotees
Keep your write up in their disable insight.

SUPER MOON

Oscillation of Super Moon in the vast swamp water
Veiled procession moves on earth –
Thousands of stars are murdered
Irresistible dark is revealed here!
The world is looking at its empty space of heart.

Nevertheless, the light descends in
the green-valley of emotional heart
Wild clouds standing silently beside the moon,
Ribbons of memory are tied on the Travelers' hand
Magical Offering is in the
audience-chamber in the dark land!

The super moon oscillating on
the water of neighbor's pond
A sportive traveler smiles boundless, from time to time
On the deluge of silvery light lovely Bakkhali flows on
On faraway in the city, brownish
Gardener is perplexed.

There's hide and seek in the arena

of the moon, destitute gloom
Darkness merely smiles, deep
darkness lies on beside it,
The birds are awake and fly whole
night among the marshes
The buds of happiness come
slowly through both heartlands

The episodes of blue dragonfly
remain unfinished, left something more
Dwelling houses in the south, behind
the dream-bound stone.
A solitary gypsy decorates the night with flower
 The Flower-bird flies, goes
and comes back - boundless.

DELUGE OF FRIENDSHIP

There's autumn decoration in the American suburb,
Ah! A Neighbor comes to immigrant's abode
In the friendship day, in the folds of Maple leaf
The festive courtyard opens atrociously.

On the wooden parapet, in the mid of railing
Hanging uneven dresses-tapestries
Get back lives, neat and tidy lively appearance.
Cuban neighbor, speaks out in Spanish tone, asks,
Who's there? Why you're
drawing the threads of remorse stare?

Here hang memories of the Third World
Keeping frank disposition in the side of adversity
Lovable white undergrowth float
under sun-drenched water;

With the touches of these leafy-cling words
The coffee cups shiver on the bends of her fingers.

Like a day when Shapla bloom with touches of kiss,

two pairs of eyes dilute in love
In the deluge of friendship float coppery cheeks,
On the bright Autumn day, rays of the sun are fugitive!

Intensive dissolution of developing index
Affection of ebb-tide love rises
in this American suburb.

HEART-RENDERING BELL

In the auditorium of Sunflower School there're
colorless photograph;
On the left stands a pair of eyes full of human stories
Inani-forest on the head, on the charming neckline
Lies a unique chignon.
In the fingers of her left hand
A piece of eroded chalk
The face of the blackboard has contrast of Kash flower
It is smeared on the duster clinched in her palm.

Wiped out fascinated memories, returns
in the layers of sensual feelings.

Ringing of the Heart-rendering Bell
is heard in the peon's hand
The school courtyard fills with rays
of newly emerged sun
The song of the emotional red and green.

The lotus-pond on the south;

A lovable bird swam
On the image of shivering water
In the north green grass-orchard-shrubs
The Golpata-thatched hut.

The evening creeps in just like footsteps of cats
Smooth paintings of hidden love
Inside the un-opened envelope.

IN THE BEAUTEOUS LAND

In the time of voyage, in the blue faraway place
Flying an appealing bird. Blended with
the smell of straw
A mural of thirst for life hangs at the end.
In this transitory life, Illusion
of the universe captivated in the palm
Huddle of the day curdle on among the couple
The island-people have thread and twinning wheel
with their Soiled hands,
endure hunger under their hands.

On the pier, the market of homebound people
gradually develop in the turnings of their life --
Ongoing morning prayers with the limpid hands.

From time to time, still under the star-scorched sky
When the lonesome heart is found,
Memories turn back to old house
The appealing bird comes back to beauteous land.
Fireflies cover the deep-drawing shades of the well
Bakkhali River is raising his waves bent to bent.

CROSSING THE OTTAWA RIVER

A Dream ferry on the water of Ottawa River
Extends its hands looking towards opposite shore
Wearing the jacket of water all the memories
Of dynamic life are floating in the flow.

Passed through the Ottawa city to that
village of Québec
The sunshine tied up, spreading out
in the open ground.
Wild birds are tweeting, heart is beating
Ancient hankie of beauty is drowning deep in the river.

Playing mind-blowing flute in the
mystery early morning
A Landless traveler knocking door to door.

FARMER

Starving for some days, a known
voyager came walking down
Beloved one looked back in the harvesting time.
The farmer sleeps with tired pleasure at dawn
Subdued sight at the nightlong love-making,
The border of Sari lying silently near the bed.

The simple life goes on flowing
with charming feelings!
Soil-clad body is ringing a tune,
A splash of rain- soaks the interior
Strenuous beauty is played in the heart!

The seeds were planted in the
era of monochrome decade,
With the touch of rain water,
All the sprouts are again rejuvenated,
Opens all its knots.

Sucking up the nectar of Rangchita,
beside the Maduna pier

The dragon-fly sleeps keeping its wings in right-angle.

The sound of saw is heard in the heart
at the fragrance of bloom
The Flower-birds are flying and inviting the spring.

PANDORA'S MISTAKE

The drunk was walking in the new moon night
The trees were deserted under the poisonous axe.
The Golden Crop is washed out in the flood
The evil party is looking for the abode
of good-hearted people.

The wheel of festivals moves through the dark road,
The face wrapped in handkerchief
under the old bridge.
If the wind is forceful the trees shrink up
The leaves shiver with the lashes of hurricane!

The parasites grow up on the unruffled tree
Poisonous seedling grows in silt-covered cropland
With the loss of leading-son the boat sinks,
Clock of progress is running reverse.

If the veins are snatched out, will the heart dance?
The clouds cannot reach the mountains!
The waves come, and the waves
go to the abode of fishes

If the crocodile calls out in the house the fish die.

Sinful people moves to the city
due to Pandora's mistake
Look! the vultures smile in the estuary!
If the Middle Age returns the darkness prevails
Fertile grounds will be submerged.

The feelings accepting the color of time
All the welfare prayers are ill-matched
Now-a-days, the darkness prevails
in the pleasant country
Destruction in the islands, humiliated with shame.

CONTINUAL OBLITERATION

White-black note - 'Is there anyone happy'?
The dead body is lying in front of the crowd
Light of comfort goes out in the vast meadow
What damage goes on in the house and away today!

The pictures of the carving poetry
are obliterated regularly
The damsel of the village did not come back again
The thief remains awake in the bun of the forest
Shall the brave boy return?

The traveler overlooked the road in the touristic realm
All over the fair are thick darkened
Bucolic spreads- the dead person laughing
The ambassadors of peace rob of all writings.

Born as human beings! if it's true
The stain of truth is in the heart, shall not erase.

CREATION

If you go ahead a few more steps
Tiredness will drop down with
tender and soft sunshine
With fulgent moonshine in the appealing night
A complete initiation.

During the harvest festival after the midnight
A valiant guard stays beside you
Gardenias are tied up and incline
Between your chignon and neckline.

Sowing with trustworthy support
subtle Oscillation of universe
Fearless eye-lids smear with Kajal of beloved one.

[Translated by Siddique Mahmud]

MONIJA RAHMAN

Date of Birth: 9 March

Place of Birth: Dhaka, Bangladesh

Education: Master of Social Science

Publication: 11

Lives in: New York, USA

Email: monija.rahman90@gmail.com

I GO NO WHERE

I could not become anyone's enemy
You need to be ruthless to have enemies
I never had it in me
The ones who considered me as their enemy
Respect me subconsciously.

I could never get close to someone
I could never master the art of
winning the hearts of millions.
Unmindful me
I can search all day long,
I find the old one while searching something else
Then I lose it again
And look for a new one!

I could never become a speaker
The real matters kick in me after the speech!
While a bohemian at heart
I could never become a bohemian
rural folklore musician.
Every plan cracks up in the middle

Of my journey

Then make the whole city stand still

And I think

I think

I think

Was I supposed to go somewhere?

MAGICIAN

Sudden meet with so many faces here and there
Only can't find my magician anywhere!
I left home ages ago
to flee with my magician,
Can anyone be in themselves?
When they are bewitched in the bones!

I stepped out ages ago
and travelled so many paths, river, jungle…
yet, couldn't find my magician!
How am I supposed to find the one
Who utters the magic spell and vanishes in thin air!
I got back after travelling so far
Happiness in my heart, even
without meeting the magician
Why do I need to search the magician outside?
While he lives in my heart!

LOVE STORED IN NATURE

I once, stored a few songs
 In the chest of Mother Nature
 I was in a fiery separation
as my heart was bleeding profusely

Once, that song was sang
whistled as a wagtail
with the calling of a Cuckoo,
stitched with dove's melodious tune in a solitary noon!

Amnesiac you got all memories back
listening to that song!
With the light of the last evening of autumn
While witnessing the dropping of orange leaves,
You felt a bit sad
After thinking of me
For the first time in your life.

DESOLATE

The girl remained desolate, forever

Flood, drought, epidemic came, one after another!

Days went on, months went on

Came a new year

Came recession

Yet, no unknown farmer came!

Yet, the girl was in heat, to be cultivated

May be, this is life

Sleepless night passes facing off calamities

The clock screams

Tic toc, tic toc, tic toc...

Breaking the silence of the night

seven train runs by

Before falling in sleep

She dreams of him

being awaken, she thinks of him,

He is that unknown farmer

for whom the girl awaited

and became desolate, forever!

BEHIND THE MASK

Behind the mask

there are also tears

Mask is a deceit

Fails to hide cunningness

Hides the mark of sadness

You were born long before

the afternoon you talk about.

In my heart

When green lemon leaves used to spread fragrance

With the thick shade of evening wind,

You came and saw my tough mask

Could not smell the soft fragrance of green lemon leaves?

You did get not know about the heavy rain falling all night

after the dark fell.

WARMTH

Surprising warmth is felt

seeing an abandoned handkerchief

Full bloomed red roses

brings absolute tranquility

in every cell of my brain

I stand before the rose garden

watch over them steadfast

green leaf, spines

snowflakes on the petals

while breathing the cold air

I realize

no one will ever

give me these roses

No one will stand by me,

carrying the warmth of that abandoned handkerchief

no one will hug me tight with all the love in their hearts,

no one will embrace with a long kiss,

when upper-lower

both of my lips are gone.

MEMORIES OF YESTERDAY

Yesterday was good day
We didn't talk
but we meet,
We had some memories of yesterday.
Today's pale clouds in the sky
will remain for some days,
we won't meet for some days
days will pass remembering the memories.
Yesterday was a good day
we didn't talk, but we meet.

There were so many people around yesterday
And was the scorching sun above
In that madness around
had the chance to see him.
Everything is intoxicated today with that gusty wind
The roads and streets are empty,
the memories fly with the cold wind.

The wait is delayed,
Today turns tomorrow

Tomorrow turns to the day after

But we do not meet!

Months passed without meeting

Passed the entire year,

Yesterday' sweet little memory from long ago

becomes life's only savings.

PAIN OF GREEN LEAF

A green leaf born
from my sadness.
My sadness flows
like chilled snowflakes!
Leaf turns into tree
tree turns into vast woodland
only sorrow lingers;
lingers the strings of un-understanding,
sorrow grows with the harshness of life!
I can't find time
to sit down with sorrow.
Yet, I made my home with sorrow
sorrow is my world.

Wearing the mascara of joy
I flee
I am a merchant
in the market of life
I wipe down tears
from my chin

In the end
I come back home in the evening
and sprinkle sorrow
onto my green tree.

LANGUAGE

These strings of sadness live deep inside my heart
He will never read them, I know!
He does not know,
my language for expressing feelings.
My roots
or in which language I dream!
He does not know
in which language I listen to songs
when my eyes are filled with tears!

Neither he is from far, nor from near.
not unseen, or seen either!
He is a stranger in an undefined relationship.
He goes around seeing the seas in holidays,
hikes around hills,
He talks about his adventures,
talks about his tanned skin!
He does not know stories about
hearts burned in anguish.
He only goes saying
and continuous saying

from the sound of the very first
sip of the morning coffee
to the restless sound of trains
he hears nothing
by hearing everything!

He understands nothing of the signs in my eyes
he does not understand the alphabets
of the watermark made of tears
left on the dried scar my cheek.

IN THE BOISHAKHI CARNIVAL OF DHUPKHOLA

No one ever wanted to know

why I like to live in a dump?

why do I love the mob

why I love turbulence!

Why solitude

exhausts me?

Why do I get depressed with

the stridulating of crickets, gallinule's clucks

no one ever wanted to know.

No one wanted to know

why I stand still,

when passing the Chinese shop,

why I love the fish stink carried by the air!

I could never say to anyone

about the fish market in Katherpole,

the buzzing of flies

the high-volume bargaining of customer-salesman

when comes down like fluttering waves

I take a deep breath

in my brain-sea

and I spread intoxicated memories in the air.

In the damp walls of pursuit
I look for the marking
in the allies of Jackson Hight's.
Why do I belong in these allies
could never say to anyone,
why do I feel like crying my hearts out
in the middle of a lonely noon!
No one could ever know,
every night in my dreams
I hear a tandem car.

A tandem car made of clay
making noise in its path
A girl pulls it with a rope
Her face is brightened with joy
She walks down holding her Dad' finger
In the Boishakhi Carnival of Dhupkhola.

[Translated by Imran Khan]

THE END